PENTIMENTI

PENTIMENTI

Selected Memoirs

ALISON ARMSTRONG

To order additional copies of this book, contact:
Xlibris
1-888-795-4274
www.Xlibris.com
Orders@Xlibris.com
781859

CONTENTS

ACKNOWLEDGEMENTS

M ANY THANKS ARE due to various people in my life who created occasions for adventures, both mental travels and physical ones. Their importance in my life will be evident in these three re-compositions.

--AA July 4th 2018
New York City

IN SEARCH OF SAINT ATTRACTA:
HYDE & SEEK IN THE WEST OF IRELAND

📖

[Below are materials for a talk given at Columbia University, February 1991; selections were then delivered as talk to American Irish Historical Society November 7, 1994. Revised and sent to Warwick Gould for *Yeats Annual,* Oct. '96 where my TSS, with several original photos, was lost. A shorter version was delivered as "Adventures in Textual Scholarship" with Powerpoint illustrations during the "Taste of Yeats Summer School" conference at Glucksman Ireland House to the W.B. Yeats Society of New York, May 12, 2018.]

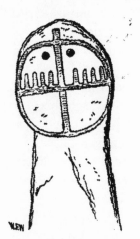

FIG. 59.—Cross at Kilturra.

It is 27 inches in height,

M Y SEARCH FOR Saint Attracta is as yet unresolved, an adventure inadvertently begun in the mid-1970s and which may never be completed, given the nature of the Irish people, of Irish Saints, and of my self. But I've had a longing to return to complete my quest for evidence: a single, uniquely carved, stone, the Cross at *Kilturra*, as I first saw it in Fig. 59 in Wood-Martin's *History of Sligo, Vol III* while reading in the Royal Irish Academy in Dublin in the 1970s. In September of 1991, I returned to the West of Ireland alone and with the sole purpose of continuing my quest. I got physically closer to my goal, it seems, yet more mired in the vagaries of memory and anticipation, of facts and fancies, of books on mythology and history.

My search is the sort of scholar's adventure which begins as a minor diversion during pursuit of the main goal (a thesis, a book) It was a project sprung from the brow of my main enterprise, to turn the manuscript materials of William Butler Yeats' late play, "The Herne's Egg," into a post-graduate thesis at Oxford with Richard Ellmann as my supervisor. My task was to work in the National Library of Ireland, Kildare Street, Dublin, before returning to Oxford to transform my pencilled transcriptions and notes into typewritten pages that would be bound. An entity in itself this project took me further afield than intended, and how could I ignore the series of coincidences, of serendipitous discoveries that balanced the more serious clear-cut process? How could I deny a "right brain" adventure running parallel to the "left brain" duty? I was, after all, in Ireland.

Perhaps my own enthusiasm for what I seemed to be finding was akin to Yeats's, the challenge to "hammer into Unity" a statement, a discovery, a coherence, out of the ephemeral stories and placenames, the texual, oral, and geographical clues which, in Ireland especially, can never be absolutely brought into focus out of the shifting mists of the past. If Ireland "hurt" Yeats into poetry, it also seduced him; and this lure of the ephemeral and duplicitous affects me, too, not to produce poetry so much as to abandon my desk and tramp the boggy fields with tools and camera as well as pen and paper.

The National Library of Ireland

Thus, in Dublin, in the summers of 1976 and 1977, while I was working in the NLI on my transcription of the manuscript of Yeats's late play *The Herne's Egg* for my Oxford thesis, I became curious about the origins of the names of Yeats's characters: Congal and Attracta. One sunny afternoon I left NLI where I was painstakingly examining Yeats's handwriting, wearing prescription sunglasses and holding up his notebook leaves so that light shone down through the paper from the skylights above my little desk in the manuscript room. An important aspect of this effort of textual scholarship was to decide which of the many crossings-out were made in which order -- and what words lay hidden beneath. Albumen prints and microfilm were useless.

And so I left the National Library and walked over to see Ide ni Thuama, sub-librarian at No. 19 Dawson Street, The Royal Irish Academy, for what I thought might be a quick look into a book or two on ancient Irish names. After the formalities of gaining admission, I spent that afternoon, and many more, for I discovered a number of tomes with references to various Congals, but more interestingly to a Saint Attracta, variously spelled.

Her name seemed so appropriate to the play's plot; Attracta, as one of a series of mortal priestesses to the Great Herne (or Heron), is not only "attracted to" or devoted to care of the Herne's rockery and his eggs, but she is also raped by seven reluctant soldiers who are ordered by their commander to be "attracted." Ironically, this ritual rape occurs not because of her feminine charms but in Congal's patronizing attempt to "do her a favour in making her all conscious woman" and thereby wreak revenge upon the Herne by "melting down" the "snows" of her virginal devotion to the bird-god whose eggs they covet but are forbidden to eat. [Incidentally, who or what lays all those eggs? Where are the female hernes?]

I found sources from which Yeats might have taken the name Attracta as well as the name of his hero, the leader of the reluctant rapists: Congal, King of Connaught.[1] I read there was a Saint Congal, Abbot of Iabh-na-Livin, at the upper part of Lough Erne; his disciple Saint Blaan who went as Bishop among the Picts in Scotland, died c.446, thus placing Saint Congal in the 3rd-4th century. But there is a more obvious source for Yeats's hero as well as for the plot of his play, one which I would come to understand better once I was back the Bodleian to read three early epics.

During my Dublin work on the Yeats manuscript in NLI, I was travelling with a friend who studied contemporary Irish literature and had recently received his Ph.D. from UConn. Sean's family owned a cottage near Ballaghaderreen in Kilcolman, County Roscommon, Connaught, where we spent much of the summers of 1976 and '77 when not pursuing our Yeatsean and Joycean interests in Dublin. Their cottage, it turned out, is very close to a SAINT ATTRACTA'S WELL! I was astounded at the coincidence. For years after, I was to recall it as being just down the "bohereen" (little road) which leads through the field to where the cottage sits high up near their peat bogs and close above Tullamore Rock, the very spot, as I would read back in the RIA, on which Saint Patrick purportedly converted Attracta to Christianity and she took the veil of a nun. According to the neighbors, and some of the texts I was soon to read on my return to the Royal Irish Academy, this occurred after she had built two stone causeways in two nearby lakes in her girlhood long before she went on to become Abbess of Boyle. The "Irish facts" which I had been told in the West of Ireland

ALISON ARMSTRONG

were semi-confirmed and elucidated -- or at least expanded upon -- in the books at the RIA and in Bodley.

Add to "Irish facts" the fickleness of one's own memory and sentiment, and we have an adventure; as our search for Saint Attracta brought us into a clearer notion of herself as a person, she yet became more elusive -- indeed, there seemed to have been **two** Saint Attractas (with variant spellings) and two respective saints' days, in addition to the two causeways, and the two holy wells.

That this adventure is beyond the call of the scholar's duty may be true, and yet one wanted to do justice to the richness of Yeats's imagination which was triggered by the name and the rocky lakeside places associated with Attracta's legend. And so we followed our noses in search of the elusive evidence and of Yeats's responsiveness to the idea. That there may have been more than one Attracta is also echoed in his having his character Attracta state that she is one of an infinite number of such "priestesses" to serve an immortal beast-god.

The characters in this play are "types" or "functions." Soldiers are secular in opposition to the sacred; or, in Yeats's terms from *A Vision*, the "Objective Primary" tincture opposes the "Antithetical." There are heirarchies within each: Congal (and Aedh his partner/opponent and their soldiers); The Great Herne (and his priestess and her servant Corney and donkey on wheelsl ("like a toy"), and three maidens whom she advises about marriage. The rational "objective" modern soldiers confront the irrational "subjective" ancient bird-god, are frustrated in a dialogue with the god's priestess who denies them the herne's eggs for their banquet; they steal the eggs, hold a banquet, but a hen's egg mysteriously appears before the hero Congal. He kills Aedh over it in a drunken rage, thus breaking their tradition of perfectly matched battles. The men then blame to Great Herne and hold a mock trial accusing Attracta of deceiving them for her god, and they take turns to *reluctantly* rape her [out of their sense of justice, not lust].

The next day Attracta denies that she was raped but claims that her god visited her in the night and consummated their sacred union [echoes of *Leda & the Swan*]; a prophecy is recited: that the hero (Congal) must die at the hand of a fool; he tries to outwit the prophecy by killing himself in the presence of the Fool and at the moment of death realizes that he himself *is* the fool; as he expires, the donkey's braying is heard by Attracta who orders her servant Corney to lie with her [echoes of a Tibetan tale based on the belief in reincarnation]. But he is reluctant out of respect for her status as priestess; she, her selfless act thwarted, states that if they had not hesitated she might have conceived and rescued the soul of Congal who now must be reborn as a donkey because **her** donkey [the reincarnation of a previous "highwayman" who presumably, like Congal, had tried to raid the herne's rockery] is copulating in the field, an idea from Alexandra David-Neel's books on Tibet. All takes place under a smiling painted moon. Yeats' daughter Ann told me in an interview at Dalkey that she had painted a backdrop to the play when it was produced in the 1950s by the Mercury Players of Lord Longford.

As you may imagine, this is a "tragi-comedy" of Yeats' late years and one that has had some problems, over the years, getting produced.

SAINT ATTRACTA OF CONNAUGHT

The prototype for Yeats's heroine Attracta in *The Herne's Egg* (published 1938) may well have been the actual Saint Attracta of Connaught, Abbess of Boyle who, according to John Colgan's *Acts of the Saints*, took the veil from Saint Patrick,[2] who lived in the 4th-5th centuries and is thought to have returned to Ireland in his missionary role some time between 432 and 456 AD. As with so many of what Hugh Kenner calls "Irish facts," I found contradictions all along my path. Even after I had finished my thesis and left Oxford I found further contradictions. For instance, John Delany's *Dictionary of Saints*[3] states that Attracta "probably lived in the next century after Saint Patrick." Donald Attwater, in *The Penguin Dictionary of Saints* has:

> "Attracta, nun. Fifth or Sixth cent.(?)...no reliable information about the Irishwoman St. Attracta (Araght). According to her legend she fled from home and was given the veil of a nun by St. Patrick at Coolavin; she then settled by Lough Gara, founded a shelter for travelers at that place, now called Killaraght. Other references suggest that she lived in the 6th rather than the 5th century...surprising miracles were attributed to her."[4]

And Laurence Flanagan, in *A Chronicle of Irish Saints* (Belfast: Blackstaff Press, 1991) says:

"Attracta [Adrochta, Athracta] of **Killaraght,** Co. Sligo (the well near Boyle was in Sligo, now in Co. Roscommon, while the well at Ballaghaderreen was in Co. Mayo and is now in County Roscommon.)

"Attracta's father was Talan, a native of Sligo. When she reached a age her father sought to engage her in marriage but she...was intent on pursuing the religious life...she set off from home with a maid called Mitain and a servant-man... in search of St. Patrick. She and her companion Mitain were both received into the religious life byPatrick. As he was consecrating them, a veil fell from heaven on Patrick's breast and he presented it to Attracta. Her modesty led her to demure and to suggest that her companion would be a more suitable recipient, which convinced Patrick that the veil was indeed intended for Attracta, and he placed it on her head.

"Although she would have preferred a site near Drumconnell, where her brother Connell had a monastery, Patrick established a nunnery at the place, later to be known as Killaraght, to which Attracta added a hospital, and he left her to rule over it.... At the behest of King Bec, she destroyed a fearsome monster by thrusting a cross into its jaws. She restored life to a drowned bard; used deer instead of horses to draw a load of timber, and strands of her own hair, instead of rope, to tie the timber to the wagons. Of her community the only physical remains are her cell, cross and well [is he referring to the well near Ballaghaderreen, Toberaracht at Kilcolman?] at which stations were still performed within living memory."

He seems to conflate the abbey at Boyle (a large site much of the outer walls which is still standing) with the site near Ballaghaderreen; this entry is accompanied by a sketch of the well at Kilcolman--not Kilaraght--at Clogher not of the well, Kilaraght, at Kilturra, with the mysteriours Fig. 59 in Wood-Martin, that free-standing cross which is nearer to Boyle.

📖

There has also been some confusion about Saint Patrick, his date of birth, and whether there were Three Patricks. Archbishop of Tuam, The Most Rev. Dr. (John) Healy confirmed (in 1905) that Saint Patrick, born a Briton on the River Clyde in 373 AD lived to be 120 years old; "...the ancient authorities generally assign the death of St. Patrick to the year 493, ...that he was about 120 years when he died is,...the best attested fact of his entire history. [See Healy's *Appendix IV,* pp. 624ff. & p. 535 on date of Patrick's death][5]

While there has been confusion about whether there were Three Patricks (Healy clarifies the issue) there very well may have been two historical religious personages named Attracta. I read in a Tourist Board brochure that the town of Boyle (County Roscommon) was visited by St. Patrick:

> "The first definite knowledge of the town is recorded in the year 435 when St. Patrick, on a visit to the town, saw the plight of travellers for whom little or no accommodation was available. He suggested to Saint Attracta, who was then the saintly Abbess of Killarraught, that she should provide a hostel.... This she did and...South of the town...Saint Attracta founded a Church...midway between Drum and the Church of St. Columba at Assylinn. Prior to the coming of Saint Patrick, a large colony existed on the banks of the river midway between Lough Gara and Lough Key [which has two islands, Trinity Island and Church Island]"[6]

My first exposure to the idea that there was a **real** Attracta [mythical and historical] whose name could have directly informed Yeats's character began with that serendipitous occasion in 1976 while staying with the family of my friend Sean near Ballaghaderreen. I was casually told there was a Saint Attracta's well nearby. "You have to go there in person." -- only so much can be accomplished in libraries reading books. So Sean and I went to find it.

ALISON ARMSTRONG

This well, or Tobhar, on the desmesne of the O'Connor Roe family, was a short drive from the cottage. We visited, Sean took photos, I collected a sample of the water which was reputed to cure eye problems.

[NOTE the ROUND STONES AROUND TOP of the WALL]

Photo: Sean V. Golden

When I returned to Dublin and resumed reading in the Royal Irish Academy, I was thrilled to discover, first in Colgan's *Acts of the Saints*, then more significantly in Wood-Martin's *History of Sligo*, then in O'Hanlon's *Lives of the Irish Saints*,[7] and then in O'Donovan's *Ordnance Survey Letters*,[8] actual--if contradictory--references made to Attracta.

It is interesting to see John O'Donovan himself, on the spot gathering information for the Ordnance Survey Letters, begin to become aware of her.

He writes, in 1836, from:

> "...Killbeagh Parish...at the village, which is at the old church- yard, there is a well called TOBAR ARACHT (Athract) the Well of Saint Aracht or Atracta, on whose day, 11th of August, a patron is held there. Is this day the same

with that of Aracth or Atracta of Killaraght, near Boyle? What is said of S. Atracta? *[OSL/*Mayo, p. 375]

"[from]...parish of Kilcolman (Costello Baronry) -- Tobar Aracht (Well of St. Aracht) at Mr. Holme's demesne, at which a patron is held on 11th Aug. ...The NE and SE corners of the old church are still to be seen in a graveyard which lies about a quarter of a mile from Ballaghaderreen, to the N. ...A.D. 1284 the Castle of Kilcolman was razed to the earth by Cathal, son of Conor Roe, King of Connaught.

There is *another* Tobararaght at Mr. Holme's desmesne 4 miles from Ballaghaderreen on the road to Boyle, at which there is a patron held on the 11th August. [*OSL*/Mayo, pp. 378-9]

"To Thomas A. Larcom, Esq., from Thomas O'Conor, Oct. 1836: I send the name books of the baronry of Leyney, having kept a memorandum of the important places...therein. I take the old documents with me....[*OSL/Sligo*, p. 363]

"Coolavin, [now] the principality of The MacDermot, but [once] of O'Gara Croghan, village of, said to be the site of the palace of the Kings of Connaught....[*OSL/Roscommon*, p. 215]...Boyle...Coolavin, principality of O'Gara. [*OSL/ Roscommon*, p. 216]

Photo: Sean V. Golden

well is surrounded by a low wall of modern masonry, with a
flat coping. On the top of the north wall are placed thirteen
round water-worn pebbles. The number, thirteen, seems re-
markable : can it have any reference to the apostles, and one
other ? Who does that mysterious stone represent ? On this
problem the whole ceremony was probably based. In the restricted
number of the stones this relic of ancient superstition differs

Fig. 57.—Rude representation of the Crucifixion, Toberaraght.

from its prototype at Inismurray, where it is alleged that they
are in such numbers on the altar that they cannot be counted—
each person who has essayed the task differing as to the total.
    On a stone inserted into the north wall there is a rude
representation of the crucifixion (see figs. 56, 57), the slab being
about 20 inches in height by 12¼ in breadth. The figure of

Wood-Martin, *History of Sligo*

Photo: Sean V. Golden

It has been observed that, for the Irish, "...there is *continuity*, in *space and in time,* between what we call our world and the other world--or worlds. Some peoples, such as the Romans, think of their myths historically; the Irish *think of their history mythologically; and so, too of their geography.*" [emphasis mine]

This has been my experience, too. There is an unreality in the landscape, as well as in the way in which the people talk about it. Nothing is clear, nothing is simple, all seems amorphous, the land is full of the past. The local people "see" and "hear" things from another world and talk about them as normal phenomena. They warned visiting "returned Yanks" such as myself about the Pooka, described the march of the Shee up the boherreen.... I had wanted the get the **facts**, but came away with impressions, interpretations, contradictions, some "Myths and Visions in the West of Ireland" of a sort collected by Yeats and Lady Gregory.

The grandfather's ghost that inhabited our cottage would make himself known of a lonely windy night when the others were at the pub called the Fiddler's Elbow in the middle of the town square a few miles away, and I, tired of drinking and darts, had offered to stay home and tend the peat fire.

This harmless ghost dropped invisible things on you, like blobs of mashed potatoes; you heard and felt them, but could see nothing; meanwhile the grinning white face of the Pooka looked in through the tiny window and galloped away into the storm. I only went out at dawn to fetch two pails of fresh water from the little un-holy well, purified with lime, at the bottom of Tullaghmore rock. And made a pot of strong tea for my hung-over Irishmen who said it was good the car knew the way back or they'd never have made it up the bohereen.

☪

I want to briefly discuss Yeats's MYTHOLOGIES regarding his account of the MACDERMOTS and the O'GARAS a little later. For the moment, note that the following excerpt from O'Donovan's *Ordnance Survey Letters (1836-37)* recounts a tale contrary to what Yeats has recorded in *Mythologies,* [the actual situation of the O'Garas and MacDermots today.] O'Donovan recorded:

> "...friars of the Abbey of Boyle having taken their last dinner up on [Dumha na Mias] ...they were driven from the monastery...some person has written in the field Name Book that the friars were banished...by a MacDermot, 'a prince of Coolavin' and that all the friars joined in cursing the MacDermot family who have never prospered since...I have to remark that whoever wrote this...knew nothing at all about the MacDermots, for they never had an inch of Coolavin which was O'Gara's until 1691 when then ancestor of the present MacDermot of Coolavin was removed thither.... [*OSL/Roscommon*, p. 210]
>
> [from] Boyle, Sept. 23, 1836

> "...On Saturday the 17th I went to the parishes of Killaraght and Kilcoleman...The patron-day is the 11th August, St. Araght's (Athracht's) day, on which stations used to be performed at Tober Athracht, a holy well in the townland of Killaraght. ...she commenced making a passage across Lough Gara, at Eanach Mhic an Aroo (Anuagh townland)... which she continued to the distance of about 3/4 mile towards the Co. Roscommon. She used to carry immense stones in her petticoat, and was seen one day by a man who was passing in a boat, and who began to admire her half stripped (naked) legs; this caused her to abandon the work through shame. They sayit is yet passable as far as it goes, resembling the Eel-Wier. However, they believe it to be the work of nature. In fact, this and other such causeways were built by prehistoric lake-dwellers.

[These local nonsense stories are dulled by the only partly glimpsed and imperfectly understood actual events and those Neolithic, Bronze and Iron Ages, and early Christian folk who peopled the land, and who still abide.]

> "She then went to the Failins in Kilcolman Parish at the Lower Lake and commenced the same work, but which she only ex- tended to the distance of 1/4 of a mile, when

she was inter- rupted by the same cause as before. She then relinquished the undertaking for ever. This latter piece of work is also still visible. Tobar Athracht is described in the Name-Book...Clochan Atracht is the name of an island in Lough Gara (north part) near Mr. McDermott's house in Shroof Town- land. There is another Clochan Athracht in the s[outh] part of the lake, Oillean na bPriochan [Isle of the Pipers??] is the name of another of the islands of the lake adjoining Clochan Athracht [Clogher is Irish for Stones -- thus: Attracta's Stones or Cell is its name]. Oilean na g-Cloch [Isle of Stones], another so-called because there is not a blade of grass to be seen being stony ground." -- signed P. O'Keefe, *OSL*/Sligo, pp. 233-38]

Note the flexible sense of time, in "pulling forward" prehistoric or pre-Christian placenames and people and mixing them with, or explaining them in, historic/Christian terms. The Celtic tendency noted above to mythologize history and geography was constantly in evidence.

This practice of mixing pagan and Christian beliefs is still strong in Catholics I met in the countryside. Our neighbor further up the hill told me (in 1976) with a straight face that she saw a procession of the Sidhe or fairyfolk marching with lights across the lower field where there is a small passage grave, and she said a prayer to keep them from doing harm to the cattle. This same summer I learned from Sean's mother that it is believed that dead relatives return as household pets. As late as 1977 (and still today, for all I know) prayers were said at the holy wells and bits of colored rags tied to the thorn trees which always grow next to them.

A man near Lough Gara told [John O'Donovan] he heard of a tradition that there was in the lake an enchantress sister to Ke (Cibh), Carrabhach and Leib; he...believed it was Athracht ni Mhannain. She went to a sick woman who lived near the lake, and asked her could the doctors do nothing for her; ....The enchantress went out and brought in an herb, and gave it to the sick woman, assuring her that it would cure her. The sick woman used it medicinally, and it had the desired effect. The enchantress asked the sick woman whether she knew her; she said she did not. 'Why, then, I'm a neighbour', said the witch, 'I live in the lake, and am going to visit my sister Ke, in Lough Ke, and cannot delay; I am allowed to see her only every seven years." [*OSL/Sligo*, p. 420]

Yeats's familiarity with the Connaught myths and geographical landmarks associated with Saint Attracta (Abbess of Boyle) most certainly originated in his visit, April 13th - May 1st in 1895 at Ratra House near the town of Frenchpark, County Roscommon, the country home of Douglas Hyde whose father was the last to inhabit the castle on the island in Loch Ke.

Hyde's house was at a place where the border of Roscommon meets those of counties Mayo and Sligo -- borders that have been shifted somewhat since. [Hence, Wood-Martin's *History of Sligo* includes the description of the Attracta's well at Kilcoleman which is now in County Roscommon. Frenchpark is on the road between Boyle and Ballaghaderreen, the road that passes both Lough Gara and Loch Key.]

Douglas Hyde, as Irish scholars recall, was an extremely learned man influential in literature and politics; poet, Gaelic scholar and one of the founders of the Abbey Theatre, he was born in 1860 in the Rectory at Frenchpark. After an academic life in Dublin he retired from his professorship in Modern Irish at UCD and went to live at Ratra House which had been bought for him by subscription. He was recalled to Dublin to become first president of the Republic of Ireland (1938-45). He is buried in Frenchpark churchyard (now a Douglas Hyde Museum, as I discovered on my most recent trip there, in September 1991). Of his visit, Yeats (then thirty years old) writes in his *Autobiographies:*

> "The man most important to the future [of the projected Celtic mystical movement] was certainly Dr. Douglas Hyde [he had founded the Gaelic League two years before, in 1893]....He once told me, when I paid a brief visit to him ...that I was the only man from Dublin who had ever stayed in his house....[10]

In Book III, "Hodos Chameliontos," of *Autobiographies,* Yeats relates:

> "When staying with Hyde in Roscommon, I had driven over to Lough Kay [Ke], hoping to find some local memory of the old...Tumaus Costello, which I was turning into a story....I was rowed up the lake that I might find the island where

he died; I had to find it from Hyde's account in *The Love Songs of Connaught,* for when I asked the boatman he told the story of Hero and Leander.... Presently, we stopped to eat our sandwiches at the 'Castle Rock', an island all castle....The roof was still sound and the windows unbroken. The situa- tion in the centre of the lake, that has little wood-grown islands...is romantic.... I planned a mystical Order which should buy or hire the castle, and keep it as a place where its members could retire ... for contemplation, and where we might establish mysteries like those of Eleusis...and for ten years to come my most impassioned thought was a vain attempt to ...create ritual for that Order. I had an unshakable conviction...that invisible gates would open as they opened for Blake ...for Swedenborg... for Boehme, and that this philosophy would...set before Irishmen...an Irish literature which...would...turn our places of beauty of legendaryassociation into holy symbols. I did not think this philosophy would be altogether pagan...."

And later in life Yeats writes:

"I meant to initiate young men and women in this worhip which would unite the radical truths of Christianity to those of a more ancient world to use the Castle Rock for this...it was in my thoughts, as much as in my writing, to seek also to bring again into imaginative life the old sacred places...to be Maud Gonne's work and mine...."[11]

Yeats *as* Great Herne, Yeats *as* a new type of Saint Patrick, in a retroactive conversion back to the pre-Christian Ireland?

Here we have in his own words intimations of the emotional importance which such a setting had for the young Yeats and was carried (as his strong feelings so often were) into mature writing. In *The Herne's Egg,* we can see the more than four decades of semi-articulated desire, and that Yeats himself is implicit in the figure of The Great Herne, while Maud Gonne would have served the function of Attracta; Maud's martyred military husband John MacBride would be Congal who had endless battles with his traditional foe.... This "family romance," of course, is only one sub-text of this strange play.

Yeats's dream of creating an Irish equivalent of the Eleusinian Mysteries in an unoccupied castle in the middle of Lough Key, one of two lakes associated with landmarks reputedly created by Saint Attracta, was never realized except in imaginative form, forty-three years later, in *The Herne's Egg.* Where Maud Gonne failed him, Attracta served.

EPIC SOURCES

The implicit chronological time of the play is 5th -7th century when Ireland was in transition from Druidic to Christian belief.

The plot and some of its characters are based on the epic poem ***Congal*** (1872) by Sir Samuel Ferguson which, in turn, was based on two early epics, ***The Banquet of Dun na nGedh*** and ***The Battle of Magh Rath*** written by Gilla-Bridghe MacConmidhe in Irish in the 15th century but recounting 7th century events -- the battle occured in 638 AD. The epics were translated into English by John O'Donovan and published in *Miscellany of the Celtic Society* (Dublin: Hodges & Figgis, 1851).

The hero of these *Sagen* is Congal-Claen, a heathen; his enemy the Ardrigh or high king is Christian. Yeats models his Congal on the heathen protagonist and the arch-rival Aedh, king of Tara, on the Christian Ard-Righ. Evidence that Yeats's interest in these sources preceded his visit to Douglas Hyde by a few years is confirmed in his youthful article, "Bardic Ireland," published Jan. 4, 1890, in *The Scots Observer*:

> "The bards, kept by the rules of their order apart from war and common affairs...rode hither and thither gathering up the dim feelings of the time and making them conscious. In the history one sees Ireland ever struggling vainly to attain some kind of unity. In the bardic tales it is ever one, warring within itself, indeed, but always obedient...to it High King. The *Tain Bo* [on "The Cattle Raid of Cooley"], greatest of all these epics, is full of this devotion. Later...men rose against their Ard-Righ for any and everything; one because at dinner he was [magically] given a hen's egg instead of a duck's [he means goose's]."

Yeats refers here to the crucial substitution found in both Ferguson's 19th century epic and in the 15th century account of the 7th century events when offense is taken by the hero over the mysterious substitution of a hen's egg for the coveted goose egg. **The Banquet of Dun na nGedh** [Fort of the Geese] states:

> "...then a goose egg was brought on a silver dish before every king in the house; and when the dish and the egg were placed before Congal Claen, the silver dish was transformed into a wooden one, and the goose egg into the egg of a red-feathered hen."[12]

Congal-Claen, a satellite king, is urged to rise in indignation against his foster father the Ard-Righ (High King) who was responsible for the magical egg-changing **only** in that his men had stolen the goose eggs for their banquet from Saint Erc. [Saint Erc was in the habit of standing all day -- like the Great Herne and indeed all herons -- in the cold waters of a stream. The saint -- like the Great Herne -- avenged himself with a curse which transformed the special egg into the common one.] Yeats's interest in the epic began early and was expressed, when he was twenty-one, in 1886 when he praised Ferguson in two essays [in *The Irish Fireside* for Oct. 9, and in *Dublin University Review* for Nov.] in which he discusses lengthy passages from *Congal* after relating its story to other Irish tales. Ferguson's epic, in five 'books', conveniently combines the original sagas of the banquest and subsequent battle. Yeats was well prepared with knowledge of ancient tales from the west of Ireland by the time of his visit to Douglas Hyde at Frenchpark in 1895 and thus had a context into which to work his discovery of Attracta's desmesne and his impressions of the rocky lake shores as the perfect setting for 'mystical rites'...which would culminate decades later in the play.

SETTING

In addition to tracing the sources of the names Attracta and Congal, we may ask why did Yeats choose the Herne [or heron] as the beast-god? There is possibly a Japanese inspiration: Yeats saw Japanese Noh masks in the Pitt-Rivers Museum while living in Oxford and he was strongly influence by the Noh play once he was exposed to it by Fenollosa through

ALISON ARMSTRONG

Ezra Pound. The crane, or "bird of happiness" is long-lived and a prevalent motif in Japanese art and literature and it is often confused with images of egrets and herons; Yeats may also have known that among the aboriginal Ainu of northern Japan the crane was known as 'the Marsh **God**' and that only women may perform the crane dance; this is also true among the Australian aborigines who dance in imitation of the crane.

The heron, a bird akin to the crane, is used as symbol of pre-Christian wisdom in *The Herne's Egg (1938),* but also in his play *Calvary (1920)* as well as in an early story "The Old Men of the Twilight" (published 1897, two years after his visit to Hyde) in which Yeats relates the belief that Druids who would not be converted to Christianity were changed into herons by Saint Patrick. [When I spoke with Miss Anne Yeats in Dalkey, June 1977, she confirmed that for this reason she emphasized the heron image when she painted the backdrop for the first production of *The Herne's Egg* at the Abbey (Oct. 29 & Nov. 5, 1950) by the Lyric Theatre Co.

In his Preface to *The Herne's Egg and Other Plays* (1938), Yeats admits:

> "'The Herne's Egg' was written [in Majorca] in the happier moments of a long illness that had so separated me from life that I felt irresponsible; the plot echoes that of Samuel Ferguson's 'Congal' and in one form or another had been in my head since my early twenties."

DUALITIES

Doublings occur in the landmarks and legends of Ireland. Attracta (or Tarahata) has attributed to her, **two** Saints' days [or Patron days or 'patterns']: February 9th and August 11. Attracta also has **two** holy wells in Connaught: Toberaraght [Well of Attracta] in the parish of Kilcoman also called Killbeagh or little church, in the Baronry of Leyney [derived from the Celtic god Lug or Lung; there is a Lung bridge at Ballaghaderreen] in the principality of Coolavin (overseen by 'the MacDermot' one of the few original lines of Irish aristocracy) in the Townland of Edmondstown, between the villages of Ballaghaderreen and Frenchpark, once on the boundary of the counties of Mayo and Roscommon and now in Roscommon. This is the first holy well I saw, and I recalled it for more than 15 years as being just down the bohereen (little road) within sight of the cottage at Tullaghmore Rock where I stayed with Sean's family in the mid-1970s; it is, in fact, as I discovered on my return in 1991, nearly two miles away.

These are from Wood-Martin.

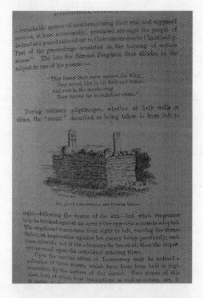

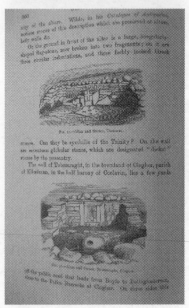

The other well, Tober Athracht (Well of Attracta) is in the Parish of Killtura (Church of the birds) also called Killaraght, near the town of Boyle in Co. Roscommon. This well is itself doubled -- the 'lost' desanctified well in the field a few meters off the road and its functioning replacement well which is right on the edge of the road. (Also, the graveyard up the road with its replaced cross -- the local family confused the old wooden cross there with the ancient stone cross I search for).

According to Colgan's *Acts of the Saints,* Feb. 9th is the Pattern Day associated with the Kilcolman well (near Ballaghaderreen); but according to O'Donovan's *Ordnance Survey Letters for Mayo, Vol. II* (1836-37), Aug. 11th was the Pattern for both the well at Kilcolman and the (desanctified) one at Killaraght near Boyle. With regard to this well at Killaraght, Wood-Martin says, in *History of Sligo:* "The 'patron' held on the 11th of August at the well [then in Co. Sligo] was abolished about the year 1776. Being on the borders of the county it was largely attended by Mayo and Roscommon people. At the close of one of these 'patrons' a faction fight occurred; a man was killed quite close to the priest's residence, and by him the annual gathering was then interdicted.[13]

RESPONSES TO THE AREA IN YEATS' *MYTHOLOGIES:*

The principality of Coolavin[14] was taken from the O'Garas by the MacDermot in 1691.[15] In *Mythologies* [compiled 1893-1925], Yeats tells a tale, "Proud **Cos**tello, MacDermot's Daughter, and the Bitter Tongue," (1897) of an ancient curse on the O'Garas -- that they would henceforward struggle and that the rival MacDermots would prosper. The story is set in the late 17th century in Coolavin, specifically between Loch Gara (Gabhra) and Loch Key (Cay).

To this day, there is an extensive O'Gara family around Ballaghaderreen, mainly working class, and "the MacDermot," still (in the 70s) Prince of Coolavin in the Baronry of Leyney [a name derived from he god Lug?]. When I was there in the summer of 1976, I met a tiny old man named John O'Gara who played darts in the country pub less than a mile down the road from Toberaraght/Kilcolman which is on MacDermot land. When I returned in September 1991, a new Douglas Hyde Museum had been established nearby in the old church where Hyde is buried in the churchyard on the road between Ballaghaderreen and Frenchpark; it is run by Mary O'Gara and is across the road from an O'Gara farm.

Earlier names around Loch Gara were Local names in Kilcolman and included Turloch. Loch-na-Nean (Lake of the Birds). Turloch, anglicized by the domineering non-Irish speaking English became Sherlock. Elder locals retold horrors the Black & Tans perpetrated on their kin -- a man dragged behind a horse to his death from that pub into the town square and dumped all broken by the steps of the Dillon house. In 1976, at the pub where we played darts with John O'Gara, there was a young man named Sherlock who thought I was Sean's former wife whom he had met years before; she is of a different race than I am, with an altogether different appearance and personality. He kept looking at me and saying, "You are surely changed, you are." I believe his confusion arose because he could not imagine a man having more than one wife.

Near the Kilcolman holy well (Ballaghaderreen), "Loch Gara Lake" is to the southwest on the road between Frenchpark and the town of Boyle, and Lough Key the Lower Lake at Failins is on the other side of Boyle to the northeast. The River Boyle, which runs through the town, connects the two lakes, each of which have stone causeways originating from prehistoric lake-dwellers. I learned this when we visited Sean's Uncle Willie, a widower who was happily remarried to a "stranger woman" from the next parish. I met Willie's elder son, Sean's cousin, who grew up on the farm near Loch Gara. In 1976 he was a London Underground policeman. Never having been encouraged to go to college, he nevertheless remained an enthusiastic amateur archaeologist who told me about his discoveries of evidence of lake-dwellers, including submerged wooden walkways in the bog. "They had them fellas out from the National Museum, from Dublin." A brochure I subsequently picked up in Boyle states:

> Recent discoveries in Logh Gara include numerous lake dwellings attributed to the Bronze Age, in which have been found many of the implements of that period. On several of the islands of nearby Lough Key, stand the ruins of ancient churches. The seat of the MacDermott family was situated on another of these islands and remains of their castle still stand.[16]

After serendipity "gave" me the Attracta's well at Kilcolman (between my the Golden's family cottage and the MacDermot estate) when I had already begun work on the manuscript of *The Herne's Egg* at the National Library in Dublin, then went to the RIA and 'discovered' the Wood-Martin description of the second well, we returned to the cottage and briefly visited Kilturra near Boyle in order to find the mysterious stone illustrated in Wood-Martin, what seemed the more interesting cross of the two wells because older, possibly 4th-5th century in origin. It combines what appears to be Ogham writing with a "Maltese cross" or "sun wheel" similar to those on ancient gold sun disks.

SAINT ATTRACTA AND THE GOLDEN PATEN

In one of the tourist brochures I picked up in Boyle is the following information under the heading St. Attracta's Cross:

> "The "Book of Armagh" chronicled the following in- cident: St. Patrick came to Ordain Priests and to conse- crate Bishops for various Missions and took the oppor- tunity to bless...[Attracta's church]. As the newly erected church was not rightly furnished, it was found that a paten had not arrived and everything else in readiness for the Saint to celebrate Mass. St. Patrick was about to defer the cere- mony when St. Attracta interposed, telling him to proceed and God would provide the missing paten....preparation for the Sacred Mysteries had hardly commenced when a golden disc appeared above the head of St. Attracta and gently rested on her shoulder while she prayed. Taking the Sacred Gift, she reverently ascended the steps and placed it on the Altar.
>
> The Paten was found to be impressed with a maltese type cross within a circle.... She said, 'It is clear that the Lord listened to thy prayers and it receives its name from thee and the Irish shall hold sanctity. We now consecrate it to the honour of God who sent it'."[17]

The image described on the paten is the very image incised on the now missing stone, for which I continue to search. Was this story concocted to account for the strange image on a small standing stone next to the well? or was the image from the gold disc or paten then carved into stone and set by Attracta's well in order to preserve that image in the memory of the Irish, for all devotees who came to her holy well? What does the encircled cross with the eight vertical incisions and two [bored?] holes *mean?* A circle containing a cross is commonly said to be a Sun Sign. Indeed, an image from heaven, or rather in the heavens. It depends, perhaps, on how much credibility one gives to miracles. At any rate, it is a unique stone, for this is what Wood-Martin said of it:

> "In the parish of Kilturra, the ancient and curious cross, situated at the well of St. Attracta, is probably of a date not later than the 6th century. It closely resembles a class of sculpture that students of ecclesiology have observed upon the walls, or over the doorways of primitive Christian Churches still re- maining in parts of Northern Africa, Syria, and Asia Minor, and these buildings are supposed to be as old as the 4th century.
>
> **"A peculiarity of this...cross is that from its horizontal limb rise eight scorings, four in each quadrant,** and in this respect the monument appears to be unique. These scorings or digits may, perhaps, be **a species of oghamic cipher**, for all writings of this *genus* were, it is alledged, intended to be more or less disguised.
>
> To the class, as represented by this specimen, no key has been at present discovered. The total height of the cross over ground is 24 inches, and it measures 10 inches along its longitudinal limb. The lines are incised in the sandstone of which the cross is formed."[18]

I felt, and still feel, an urgent need to see and touch this missing stone and have made three excursions (among other trips to Ireland) for this purpose, in '76, '77, and again in '91.... After further reading, it seems to me that this (Fig. 59) is an extremely early example of the type of incised "ringed equal-arm cross" combined with Oghamic cipher that predates the Romanesque (12ᵗʰ cent.) "High" or Celtic Cross. Not only its ringed cross (with in this case a slight longer verticle middle section that juts **above**, rather than below, but the eight Oghamic scorings above the horizontal section, would indicate that it is at least pre-700 if not earlier. It dates, I believe, from the time of transition in Ireland, between pagan druidic powers and Christian, that is, the time of Saint Patrick, the time of Saint Attracta, the time of Yeats's play "The Herne's Egg."

Douglas Hyde, in *A Literary History of Ireland,* (1899), says, with regard to Ogham,

> "...the celebrated Ogam script, ...a number of short lines, straight or slanting, and drawn either below, above, or through one long stem-line...[and in a ftnt]: Thus four cuts to the right of or below the long line stand for S, **above it they mean C....**[19] [What would C C have to do with Attracta?]

Hyde continues:

> "Ogam writing is peculiar to the Irish Gael and only found where he had settled ....[p. 109]....All ancient Irish literature, then is unanimous in attributing a knowledge of Ogam to the pre-Christian Irish [p. 112].

The earliest Christian stone crosses are equal armed (maltese) crosses, or ringed, and frequently combined with oghamic cipher. Peter Harbison, in his book *Pilgrimage in Ireland: Monuments and the People*, says:

> "It would seem to be generally agreed that the invention of the Ogham script predates the time of St Patrick in the 5ᵗʰ century, ... The numerous Ogham inscriptions

in parts of Wales and Cornwall [Note: the many holed stones in Cornwall!], where some of the Deisi tribe of County Waterford are known to have settled in around the 4th or 5th century, may have played a role in transmitting a knowledge of this Roman based script to Ireland....The use and knowledge of Ogham continued to flourish undiminished after the introduction of Christianity....Around thirty Irish Ogham stones are **known to bear a cross as well as an Ogham** inscription ...there is almost no way of knowing whether both are contemporary, because cross and inscription do not overlap to show which was earlier...."

He goes on to argue that ringed equal-armed crosses on ogham-inscribed stones all seem clearly linked with pilgrimage, which would include celebrations of Patterns, a form of local pilgrimage on a patron's day.[20]

In the summer of 1976, I found a plain well with a cement cover right in the ditch by the road to Boyle, with a barbed wire fence and rough field above; it was about a quarter-mile from the cemetery at Kilturra. No cross, no inscription, nothing but a utilitarian well whose simple concrete and stone steps and enclosure might have been made any time in the past 100 years. No moss on the steps. Nothing mysterious. It was clearly in use.

Sean and I climbed up into the field and trudged about in thick grass. Nothing. Then down the road to the nearest cottage, lime-washed pink with white trim, a corrugated roof, a very neat gravelled yard. The interior was laid out just like the Golden's cottage; concrete walls and floor, an unused parlor and dairy off on the right, two small bedrooms on the left, in the middle the kitchen, a dresser with delf, a wooden table covered with oilcloth, patterned lino on the cement floor, but with a white enamelled stove burning peat [even in the summer] with its pipe up the flue of the small concrete fireplace.

I had a chat with the woman of the house [*bean an tighe*] who was soon joined by her husband. First, the weather, then to business. Although he was a "stranger" from the next parish, he recalled an old cross. How old? "Oh, very, very old" (this gave me hope I was on the right track) and that it had been broken into three by a thunderstorm and taken away by the priest of that parish. As it turned out, they mistook an old wooden cross up in the cemetery for the stone with the incised cross which was never right on the road but next to an older, now hidden, well up in the field. They were very pleased with the new cross and recommended I should go up and see it. (I had already viewed what I considered a monstrosity which jarred both my Celto-romanticism and austere Presbyterian sensibilities). So, where was this mysterious and delicate ancient carving on a stone too short to be blown over.

When I returned to Oxford in the autumn of '76, I reached, through correspondence with Father Benignus Millet in Killiney, a Canon Mahon of St. Joseph Parochial House, Boyle, who kindly wrote and made me a present of a fat book. (It seems he thought I was a boy student.) Canon Mahon sent a letter (Oct. 17, 1976) some things I had already discovered "in the field," so to speak. He also confirmed what I had been told at the cottage; both parties, perhaps so conscious of their Roman Catholic interests that they simply were unable to see the "pagan"-looking image as having religious connections, were completely missing my point, that it was a maltese type cross within a circle *incised* on a rough stone for which I searched, what seemed to me a primitive form of "Celtic Cross" or cross within a wagon wheel:

"Dear **Mr.** Alison Armstrong [wrote Canon Mahon]

...I am not an enthusiast of Yeats ... I know what a Heron is-- a Herne I suppose means the same thing. St. Attracta's well is inside the road ditch outside of which is **another** well from which the villagers draw water. It is three miles south of Boyle on the road towards Frenchpark. Great gatherings of people used to assemble there on Saint Attracta's Feast day 12th [sic]

Aug (now the Feast of Roaring Meg in the Six Counties).

These gatherings...known as "patterns"...ceased nearly one hundred years ago because of the murder of a certain man in a faction fight. The parish of Killaraght is not mine as it is in County Sligo [and he drew a line map to show

how Killaraght is in a portion of Sligo that intrudes into Roscommon]. All Boyle parish is in County Roscommon. Many of my people are buried in Killaraght.

"The 'cross' was not blown down by storm; it was made of timber; the timber had rotted and the people of the district were afraid that it would fall and thus break the stone figure of the 'Crucified' which was nailed onto it and purchased 70 years before by their grandfathers at five shillings per family. This was two years ago [e.g., 1974]. So they looked for replacement & price to make a cross. The Nire factory in Boyle was selected and they made a Cross of steel and pre- sented it free to the Killaraght Parish. They nailed the figure of the Crucified onto it or fastened it in some other way. I was present at the blessing of the new Cross two years ago by Father James Walsh C.C., Cloonloo. The original timber of the cross was brought to the Nire factory, Boyle so it is not possible to see the original cross....

"From what I have read the Attracta of the well in Kilcolman parish is the **same** as the Attracta of Boyle. Kilcolman and Lough Gara were in the territory of her father Talan. It was characteristic of St. Patrick to contact the Princes of the territory in which he was before preaching the Christian Faith. This was good manners anyhow. We have a song 'St. Patrick was a Gentleman'.

"In regard to sources *Bibliotheca Sanctorum II*, I have the *Writings of St. Patrick* by Archbishop Healy in 1905. He was born near Boyle. I have two volumes; I can make you a present of one of them if you think it would be of any use to you. [He did send the volume which I received at my cottage on Boars Hill.]

The 'passageways' you mention were there long before St Attracta's time. They can be seen today in Lough Gara & in Lough Key. They are called 'Crannogs' in Lough Gara- -Crannogs were dwellings for human beings made of very

ALISON ARMSTRONG

tough brushwood etc. Some of their foundations are above the water; I stepped out on one some time ago and I sank and would never extricate myself only another man was near me. The people lived here for protection or perhaps to be near fishing....In Lough Key these stone underwater passages led to monasteries to which the laity could go for prayer or recollection or to do penance. (There are both causeways and tunnels.)

"I crave forgiveness for my meagre knowledge and I hope that you will get your B. Litt. *summa* cum laude. Have no scruple about writing if you think I can be of any use.

"Yours sincerely,
[signed] Thomas Mahon/ (Canon Mahon)
[PS] "'Cel Atrachta' = Killaraght."

Canon Mahon seemed totally unaware of the stone about which I had written him, as well as confused about my gender, religion, degree programme, and age. I had already seen the new tall cross that he seemed so proud of. And it was not at all by the well but up the road in the cemetery.

I had no response from anyone else (including the editor of the *Roscommon Herald*) until I received another letter from another man of the cloth, Fergal Grannell, o.f.m., who wrote to me at Oxford Nov. 11, 1976:

Father Grannell's summary of sources includes:

"Namesenchus naemh nErenn," Ed. P. Grosjean in *Irish Texts*, fasc. III (London, 1931), p. 74...[which] identifies Attracta as 'the daughter of Saran son of Caelbad son of Cronn Badhraoi, et al; while "Genealogiae regum et sanctorum hiberniae," Ed. P. Walsh in *Archivum Hibernicum* 6 (1917), Appendix p. 98 identifies her as daughter of Talan son of Saran son of Caelbad son of Cronn, etc. "Thus according to these two sources, she was either the daughter or grand-daughter of

Saran son of Caelbad. This Caelbad, son of Cronn Badhraoi (in Irish, Caelbad macCruind Badhraoi) reigned as King of Ireland for one year and was slain in 357, according to *Annals of the Kingdom of Ireland by the Four Masters,* I, *sub anno* 357, ed. J. O'Donovan (Dublin, 1851). Therefore, both the genealogists and the annalists would concur that St. Attracta lived sometime during the Fifth century, and was a contemporary of St. Patrick. The Irish Martyrologists say very little about her, except to note her feastday as 11 August. *The Martyrology of Tallaght* [21] refers to her simply in 'Feast of Etracta, virgin', while the *Martyrology of Gorman* [22] merely mentions her name as Athracht.

"The former source dates from about the year 800, which argues strongly for a body of devotion to Attracta prior to that period. The *Martyrology of Donegal* [23] also gives her name, and adds that she was the daughter of a certain Tighearnach of Cell Saile in Crich Conaill [Note: that is, she is claimed by another province than Connaught]...the placename is tentatively identified as Kilsally in the parish of Ballyclog, Tyrone [in Northern Ireland]. It would be pointless [Fr. Grannell continues] to try and reconcile the various extant and apparently conflicting details that have been recorded concerning St. Attracta. Even in medieval times, while popular devotion to her may have been strong, historians had little to say about her [which] made it all the more easy for Augustine Magraidin, the Augustinian Canon of the Island of the Saints on Lough Ree (he died 1405), when writing up the traditions as did survive in his day, to embellish them to his heart's content, irrespective of historical truth."

I was on a wild goose chase, it seemed.

That day we first drove from Ballaghaderreen and the Kilcolman well to find the Killaraght well and that missng Stone which exited me so, I was directed first to a graveyard which was set back off the road to Boyle near a crossroad. A long gravel path led from a simple iron gate through thick grass [1976, the year of the drought, was an excellent summer for hay]. At the edge of the graveyard stood a new-looking cross made of steel I-beams with a Victorian-looking stone or plaster carving of Christ crucified on it; it towered above us.

Nothing mysterious here. I was disappointed but undaunted and headed for a corner of the graveyard that appeared to be the oldest--a large dark spreading tree by a stone wall where the dark grass was long and moist despite the hot sun. I walked round and round the uneven ground, stood on a fallen gravestone to peer over the wall into the next field, saw nothing resembling an old well, stepped down and backed away and stumbled -- over a long white bare thighbone. That I was treading on someone's grave deeply impressed itself upon me, then. I quickly thrust the legbone under a bit of turf beside the broken stone and backed away respectfully. As I retreated, my sandal strap inexplicably broke -- perhaps a minor reprimand from the Beyond.

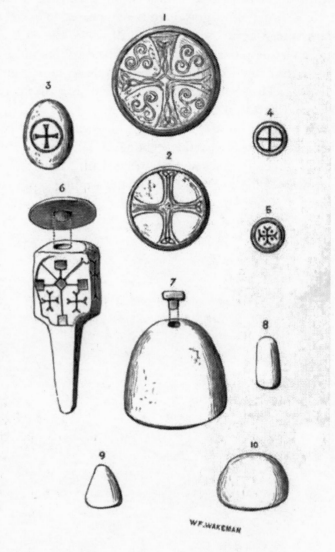

Fig. 52.—Cursing Stones, &c., Island of Inismurray.

From Wood-Martin

So, there were three wells (one at Kilcolman and two wells at Killaraght), and there were four crosses (two at Killaraght/Kilturra cemetery and one missing stone that stood by the missing well at Killaraght, and the other, at Kilcolman, set into the wall, a 17th century crucified Christ (with physical characteristics of the Sheela-na-gig) and wrought by I.G. -- an O'Gara.)

Of this well, Wood-Martin is again my most inspiring source: Along with his Fig. 56 -- Altar and stones...and Fig. 57, Rude representation of the Crucifixion, Toberaraght,

> "The well of Toberaraght, in the townland of Clogher, parish of Kilcolman, in the half barony of Coolavin, lies a few yards off the public road that leads from Boyle to Ballaghaderreen, close to the police barracks at Clogher. On three sides this well is surrounded by a low wall of modern masonry, with a flat coping. On the top of the north wall are placed thirteen round water-worn pebbles. The number, thirteen, seems re- markable; can it have any reference to the apostles, and one other? Who does that mysterious stone represent? On this problem the whole ceremony was probably based. In the re- stricted number of the stones this relic of ancient superstition differs from its prototype at Inismurray, where it is alleged that they are in such numbers on the altar that they cannot be counted--each person who has essayed the task differing as to the total.

> "On a stone inserted into the north wall there is a rude repre- sentation of the crucifixion...the slab being about 20 inches in height by 12 1/2 in breadth. The figure of our Savior (in high relief) is about 14 inches in length; the head is out of all proportion to the rest of the body, measuring 5 inches to the end of the beard, the body but 4 1/2 inches to the termination of the garment. The head is chiefly remarkable for the hair, ...the beard also being curled....The body shows the ribs,...small and badly carved; the arms extended. The cross on which the figure is suspended is in relief of about 1/8th inch from the face of the stone, and is 17 inches long from the top to the moulded base, into which the shaft is

represented and set, as in the old Irish crosses; the base is 2 inches in height. The shaft of the cross is 2 inches wide, and the arms 12 inches across.

On the right side of the cross there is a spiral carving surmounted with a rude representation of a bird--probably intended to represent a cock. There is also a ladder; the devices on the other side are a hammer, nails, &c.

Representations of the Crucifixion are relatively so few in the County Sligo, that it seems desirable to place this one on record, though it certainly possesses no unique feature, and is of comparatively recent date, as evidence by an inscription inserted at one side of the figure of the Crucifixion instead of over it, *i.e.*, I.H.S. 1662, II. I: G: The numeral after the date may signify the 2nd year of the restoration, and the initials I.G. after the date may stand for Iriel O'Gara.

"At the foot of the wall may be seen a hollow in a large boulder. The water in this was formerly believed to be a certain cure for children who were 'long in walking', i.e.... afflicted with rickets. The patron-day appears to have been the 11th August. The altar and walls were some years ago restored by the nuns of Ballaghaderreen."[24]

All this I read about and verified "in the field" back in 1976 & '77 [as these photos attest], and I've remained haunted by Attracta's wells, by the very vagueness of my "researches" that ran underground along with my more serious task of deciphering and editing Yeats's manuscript and defending my thesis and then the years of revision to prepare it for publication. For years, I carried with me a bottle of water gathered from the Kilcolman well -- not that I had rickets but in the hope it might do my overstrained eyes some good. It always stayed pure in its little shandy bottle.

In September of 1991 I returned to Ireland, rented a car, and spent 10 days driving about my old haunts (with a couple of days in Dublin) and actually got a little closer to my goal. While the well at Kilcolman has altered with neglect, I was able to find the actual remains of the desanctified well at Killaraght; it was, in fact, up in that field -- a very old man on a bicycle I met up at the cemetery talked with me; he cycled there daily to visit the grave of his wife who had died 20 years before. He said he recalled the old well from his childhood, and went with me down to the place.

We climbed over the ditch behind the new concrete well by the road, up the embankment and under the barbed wire. After a few moments of tramping the thick grass, he showed me an indentation and I set to work with my little hunting knife to cut away the turf and expose the stones that lined the old well. But still I found no standing stone, 27 inches above ground, with an incised cross within a circle. I want to go back. I will continue to write letters which may never be answered. *Is* the "face"-like image that haunts me, an image (like the paten on which this cross was inscribed) from pre-Christian times? Are the markings a form of ogham?

Establishing the identity of Attracta in Celtic mythologized history shows, at least, how appropriate a choice she is as the prototype of the "wise virgin" in Yeats's play. That he uses her name and character as well as the rocky lakeside landscape of her habitat argues in favor of his having discovered her during his visit to Douglas Hyde in 1895; this assumption is supported by his use elsewhere of other legendary material from that locale, as in Yeats' *Mythologies*.

Thus, his early visit to Hyde proved a productive one which informed his writing for the remaining four and a half decades of his life.

How much value this material has for Yeats scholarship is indeterminable, possibly marginal. However, the indirect influence that my Yeatsean pursuits have had on my creative life is profound. The uncanny sense of multiple periods of time (myth-in-history) and the spiritual awareness of an individual caught up willingly or not in natural processes that are beyond understanding became conscious for me while in Ireland through my search for Saint Attracta.

Much time went by between the completion of the thesis and the subsequent book that was to appear with Macmillan of Canada and finally Cornell University Press which had already mades its mark with the extensive series of volumes on the Wordsworth materials. Steve Parrish oversaw the Yeats volumes, we editors were given no royalties, only royalty reports, with all proceeds going toward the Yeats family. From the time of agreeing to work on "The Herne's Egg" materials, a play I had discussed in my masters thesis at Ohio State in 1972, and which I was urged to do by Richard Ellmann and the general editors David R. Clark at Amherst, Massachusetts, and Steve Parish at Cornell, the history of printing evolved from hot type to photolithography.... all out of our initial instructions to type my pencilled notes on two typewriters, pica and elite, in black or red ribbon, to indicate to the typesetter changes in Yeats' handwriting and writing materials. Eventually, back in the US, a box of books arrived in December 1992. My very own volume in the Cornell Series, but there was no one with whom to share my immense relief and delight.

ALISON ARMSTRONG

Endnotes

1   See my essay, "Prosecutors Will be Violated: Sexuality and Heroism in *The Herne's Egg*," in *Canadian Journal of Irish Studies*, IX, No. 2 (Dec. 1983), pp. 43-56. (Revised and posted on Academia.edu website, summer 2013)

2   Under "Acts of Attracta" and in "tria Thaumaturgica" in Colgan, *Acts of the Saints* (Dublin) see 5th Appendix ad St. Patrick. Cop. xiii, p. 270. See also facsimile of "Acta Sanctorum Hiberniae," Introd. Brendan Jennings (Dublin Stationery Office, 1948), pp. 277-82. The validity of Colgan is discounted by J. O'Hanlon in *Lives of the Irish Saints*, Vol. II (Dublin: Duffy, 1877).

3   (Doubleday, 19??), p. ??.

4   p. 54.

5   The Most Reverrend Dr. Healy, Archbishop of Tuam. *The Life and Writings of Saint Patrick* (Dublin: M.H. Gill & Son, 1905), p. 26; p. 535.

6   From a brochure, *The History of Boyle Abbey: Lakeland for Holidays*, issued by the Midland Regional Tourism Organisation Ltd. and printed in the Republic of Ireland by Roscommon Herald, Boyle. [n.d.], c. 1975.

7   J[ohn] O'Hanlon. *Lives of the Irish Saints*, Vol. II (Dublin: Duffy, 1877).

8   *...for the Counties of Mayo, Roscommon, and Sligo* (Dublin: National Library of Ireland, 1836-37)

9   Marie-Louise Sjoestedt, *God and Heroes of the Celts*, transl. by Miles Dillon. (Berkeley: Turtle Island Foundation, 1982), p. 11.

10   "*Autobiographies*, xiv," in *Memoires*, Edited by Denis Donoghue (London: 1972), p. 54.

11   Op cit., p. 123.

12   *Miscellany of the Celtic Society*, Ed. John O'Donovan (Dublin: Hodges & Figgis, 1851; on p. 16, the title is disputed: "In...no. 60 of Ms. collection of Messrs. Hodges and Smith, is written Dun na n-Gaedh, i.e.,...fort of the darts or wounds...[the name] does not appear to be derived from the goose eggs which are made the principle cause of the Battle of Magh Rath." If spelt *nGedh* it reads Geese; if spelt *nGaedh*, then it means darts/wounds.

13   Wm. Gregory Wood-Martin. *History of Sligo: 1691-1891* (Dublin: Hodges & Figgis, 1892), p. 371

14   See James McGarry, *Place Names in the Writing of William Butler Yeats*, Preface by Kathleen Raine, Ed. Edward Malins (Gerrards Cross: Colin Smythe, 1976), pp. 34-35. "Cool-A-Vin...Cuil O'bhFinn, the corner of the territory of

Finn, a son of Fergus Mac Roy....On the border of County Sligo and County Roscommon adjoining Lough Gara (formerly Lough Techet). Owned by the O' Gara family until the Mac Dermots of Moylurg took up residence there when they lost their lands at Lough Key. They built a house at Sroove on the shore of Lough Gara, and The MacDermot became known as The Prince of Coolavin. This is the setting erroneously given by Yeats as the home of Una NicDermot in "Proud Costello". Afterwards the family moved to a newer house in Coolavin, the entrance to which is opposite Toberaraght, St. Attracta's Well, also known as Clogher Well. ... The Barony of Coolavin is closely associated withy St. Attracta, who received the veil from St. Patrick and maintained a Hospital or house of hospitality for travellers at Killaraght. Fergal O'Gara, 17th c. chieftain of Moygara in the Barony of Coolavin, financed the authors of The Annals of the Four Masters (1632-1636)...."

[15] See John O'Donovan, **Ordnance Survey Letters for Mayo, Roscommon and Sligo** (Dublin: National Library of Ireland, 1836-37), p. 215.

[16] **Boyle: Lakeland for Holidays**. Published by Boyle Chamber of Commerce in association with Boyle Development Association with the assistance of the Midland Regional Tourism Organisation Ltd., Mullingar, and Bord Failte Publicity Advisory Service. Printed in the Rep. of Ireland by the Roscommon Herald, Boyle. Design by Sean O'Dowd [c1969]

[17] **The History of Boyle Abbey.** A Lakeland for Holidays brochure published by the Midland Regional Tourism Organization Ltd., printed by Roscommon Herald, Boyle. [n.d., purchased 1991]

[18] **History of Sligo**, p. 371

[19] pp. 108ff.

[20] Syracuse University Press, 1991, pp. 205ff.

[21] Ed. R.I. Best and H.J. Lawlor (London: Henry Bradshaw Society, 1931), p. 62.

[22] Or, **Felire Hui Gormain**, Ed. W. Stokes. (London: Henry Bradshaw Society, 1895), pp. 154-55.

[23] Published by Irish Archaeological and Celtic Society. Ed. J.H. Todd and W. Reeves (Dublin: 1864), pp. 216-17.

[24] **History of Sligo**, pp. 366-68.

MEDITATIONS OF A LADY SEA-KAYAKER

". . .if only one could film like that. . . to look
without wanting to prove anything."
--Wim Wenders, *Tokyo-Ga.*

"IN DREAMS BEGINS RESPONSIBILITY"

I ALWAYS DREAMED OF having a boat, a sailboat. I didn't admit this until my mid-forties, for this dream had been superseded in my conscious and ever-unrequited desire for a horse of my very own -- and a farm with a stone house and a barn. As a child, I stole careening bareback rides on neighbors' horses across open meadows, fractured my spine and cracked my skull from a couple of falls, had spent every hot summer afternoon hanging around the old blacksmith's shop down on Electric Street (which was nothing but a dirt road with a couple of falling down houses on it), read all the best horse stories (Walter Farley I still keep), sketched horses in all the margins of my elementary school notebooks and even in college. I "graduated" from bareback to western saddle to hunter seat without benefit of formal lessons and eventually did a little jumping (and had another couple of falls) whenever I had the time and money to take a class at a stables once I was in college and on my own. Riding rental horses under the strict eyes of various stern instructors in Ohio, then in Ireland, England, New York, New Jersey, kept me in fairly good form over the decades and kept alive the illusion that One Day My Horse Would Come. Preferably as the white Arab that haunts my more Jungian dreams. He is my totem animal. In my dreams, my horse is often running on the seashore. Not very original, perhaps, but appealing.

In 1989, during a summer of profound anxiety and depression, it was too hot to ride in Central Park, and I needed some joy to balance the stresses of completing an overdue Ph.D. dissertation at NYU and an unhappy love life. I sought refuge one evening in an adult education lecture at The Cooper Union. I taught freshmen literature courses there, so I could attend any of these evening courses free of charge.

The particular class I walked into was entitled, "Your Dreams and Creativity." Something like that. The instructor was a woman whose anthropological research on the function of dreams in "primitive" cultures could be applied to us New Yorkers. She talked about how we could not only learn from our dreams but could *direct* them toward healing our lives. She explained how each of us should get in touch with our Inner Child. On this particular evening, she had her audience do a few mental exercises. One required us to picture our Inner Child, approach her and ask what it wanted as its favorite toy or present. We were to accept the answer without judgment and then go out the next day and buy the gift, no matter what the cost.

Well, my Inner Child was playing by the seashore when I approached her in my imagination, and she knew exactly what she wanted most: a red and white wooden sailboat with real cloth sails. I was pleased with her answer and not even surprised that she didn't mention horses. I had bought such a boat for my son when he was four, and we had sailed it on Mirror Lake on The Ohio State campus long ago when I was twenty-four. He reached for it as it sailed away, then he slipped and fell into the icy water. I was terrified for his health because it seemed ages until I could find a friend to come with a car and take us home. After that, the red wooden sailboat sat on his little blue dresser. I don't know where it is now. When he went to Canada in the summers with his grandfather he got interested in motorboats. My son is grown-up, now, with children of his own. They don't sail and but one of my granddaughters is crazy about horses.

Other, earlier, memories of sailboats, real ones, come to mind: my Uncle Woody's boat, a Lightning, which he kept on the reservoir near Mansfield, Ohio, and sailed in regattas on Sunday afternoons. He let me "crew" for him when I was twelve, along with the grown-up cousins I admired. And once, up on Lake Erie when I was perhaps thirteen, I was caught out in a terrific storm in my father's friend's somewhat larger sailboat, a Thistle, along with his son Walter and the daughter of my father's other friend Pinkie Stevenson.

This big man with the deep calm voice, sailing us from Middle Bass Island to rejoin our parents at Put-in-Bay made us aware of the dangers, the vastness of the stormy water, the need to understand the dynamics of sails and rudder with wind and water. The skill and care of my father's friend meant that we had a real adventure, survived a thunderstorm "at sea" (for the Great Lakes are like inland seas, you can't see across them, only a hazy horizon where Canada should be). We learned things that made us a little more grown-up. But somehow, I retained a feeling that such expensive and non-utilitarian activities such as sailing were for others, others better off.

But now my Inner Child insisted on her own wooden sailboat with real cloth sails. And I recalled another experience, a more recent desire. It had come to me as a dream at the end of a strenuous year during my grief at the loss of a child. I was forty-five when I had nearly become a mother again after twenty-five years. I was just four or five weeks pregnant, and yet...I was haunted by the "might-have-been" which seemed a part of what-*has*-been, the "real" past. In the midst of my despair and loss, that dream was one of many positive and even thrilling visionary dreams set on the Hudson River which flows past my building, indeed, is the view from the windows of my apartment that I was offered, and gladly accepted, nine months later. (It also has a view of the spot where a dear friend of mine landed after jumping off the roof of my building some five years previously, but that is another story.) It seemed that this apartment "had my name on it." But at the time of this particular loss of the child, I was separated from my husband who was on the third floor while I was living in my studio without plumbing deep in the interior of our building, and teaching at The Cooper Union, bathing at the NY Health and Racquet Club. I was as yet unaware that I would get an apartment on the River. (I expected another two years on the waiting list.) The subsequent dream that appeared to heal me came within the first week of living in my new apartment by the River.

This dream was a consolation and a prophecy. As I stood at the concrete barrier by the edge of the Hudson River, I saw the lost child coming toward me rapidly on a shiny new red tricycle; he was clean and scrubbed and beautifully dressed, perhaps three years old with a look of complete trust on his little round smiling face. Suddenly, a big wind blew downstream, from the north, and to his surprise, and mine, he was swept away backwards despite his sturdily pedaling little legs.

He looked at me with dismay, without sadness or disappointment or reproach as he vanished.

And then I saw -- and felt -- myself sailing singlehandedly a beautiful large red wood sailboat, all its rigging and sails in order, down the river; the north wind, which had swept away the child, filled my sails. I was older, totally self sufficient, confident, mature and, what most struck me -- for I was seeing myself on my boat from the riverbank and at the same time I was me in myself sailing my boat -- I saw that my forearms and hands were very brown from the sun and very strong and sinuous and capable. I was captain of my own ship; the wind was with me, and I was sailing south in the direction that my lost child had gone. Towards New York Harbor. Out to sea.

I felt upon waking that my child had manifested itself anew in this strong relationship of sailor and sailboat rather than as mother and child, that nothing was lost after all. That this was to be simply a transformation, an awakening to new possibilities. After that dream, in January 1989, came some unexpected changes in my life

But I am getting ahead of my recollections. After hearing the lady speak on "Your Dreams and Creativity" at The Cooper Union that winter, I did go to a toy store. If we are to do justice to our Inner Child and re-integrate her, we must honor her need, the propriety of fulfilling her wish, without reservation. So said the lady at The Cooper Union that evening. I went uptown to the best toy store I knew of, F.A.O. Schwartz on Fifth Avenue. My sole mission was to fulfill *her* desire, a Real Wooden Sailboat with Real Cloth Sails. Now.

I ascended on the escalator to the mezzanine and there, among remote controlled cars and Barbie Dolls and Mickey Mouses and other irrelevant items, was a lovely dignified display of real wooden sailboats made in England. Some of these boats were immense--several feet long and sporting magnificent sails on four or five-foot masts; they cost far more than I had to spend. But the instructions were to buy my Inner Child the very best of what she wants to the very best of my ability without reservation.

I looked and looked, held and examined them all, and chose the right one. Not the biggest, which would hardly have fitted into my new apartment, but the best of the smaller ones, with a red rudder that moves, cloth gib and mainsail with brass grommets and a wooden boom, a fixed keel, a brightwork deck, white wooden hull with red stripe, and a name: *Endeavor I.* Length, approximately sixteen inches overall, twelve inches in the water. Of course, I was at that time unaware of all the correct nautical terminology. But I was doing the right thing. It felt good and slightly irresponsible. I wrote out a check for fifty-some dollars, went back down the escalator and proceeded down Fifth Avenue bearing the beautiful and perfect toy boat. I let myself be carried along by a stiff March wind and my new-found recklessness.

When you change direction even in a minor adjustment of normal activity, there may be consequences a hundredfold, especially surprises. And my neglected self re-entered into the world of action.

So, you may be wondering, When are you-the-writer and purported kayaker going to put me-the-reader on the water? When do you share the joys and thrills of deep-sea paddling, of communion with Nature, of braving the vicissitudes of maritime weather while sitting only a few inches beneath the surface of the sea with only a fraction of an inch of rubberized fabric between us and the infinitely deep, inhumanly cold and alien ocean? But wait. Meditation before action.

ZEN, SHAMBALA, SKIDBLADTHER

There is a further connection with my Uncle Woody and sailboats, an event of which I was not made aware until I had begun my own adventures kayaking and camping through the Adirondacks, by Lake Champlain, and up into Maine in August 1990 with my friend and neighbor Ken and his Klepper, a double red sailing kayak. When I telephoned my mother in Ohio from a campground near Bar Harbor on Mount Desert Island, she replied, "Why, I believe that is where Woody ended up when he sailed from Lake Erie by way of the canals and Lake Champlain to the East River and Hell's Gate and up the coast to Bar Harbor; your Aunt Ann's family had a summer house at Bar Harbor."

Why hadn't anyone included me? Why did no one tell me? Was I too much younger than my other cousins? Or perhaps no one told me these things because they thought I was just a scholar and not an outdoorsy person? The precedent set by Uncle Woody seemed yet another confirming link in a chain of events so that I felt more than ever justified in following my impulses. He had sailed with Aunt

Ann and one of my cousins, perhaps Betty, and Aunt Ann's brother had accompanied them with a motorized boat. It must have been a wonderful adventure, so much sailing in that little open sailboat.

As soon as we settled at a campsite, Ken and I explored the length of Somes Sound on several day-long expeditions and I thought of them, now, my father's older brother and his family, coming to a place where they were quite at home too; and my sense of breaking new ground, of being the "avant garde" of my Ohio family vanished. I was now an explorer; I was unknowingly following in their footsteps, confirming a family tradition. Yet, for Ken (who had already been here) and myself, we seemed to be pushing back horizons that had become too limited in the city. We moved to Sea Wall on the "quiet side" of the island, after Ken secured **B3**, the best campsite, a mossy little paradise among the tall spruce.

We stayed at Sea Wall in my new tent for two weeks. I was to leave in September to return to my New York apartment and the usual teaching at Cooper Union. I woke up early at the beginning of Labor Day week-end. As we crawled from our respective damp arthritis-inducing sleeping bags, I stated that it might be a good idea to look in the paper about my renting a house for the winter. Nobody came to Maine for the winter; houses would be cheap; I wanted to be alone. My ex-husband had died the month before and I was disoriented by a widow's grief, but also aware of the freedom that the money he left me would provide. And I had the galleys of the Yeats book to finish for Cornell University Press. Why not?

Ken and I had walked our bikes up a hill in Bass Harbor to take the ferry to Swan's Island and we passed a tiny white wooden house whose miniature bay window and doorstep were right at the edge of the road, the way so many old houses were built in the days of horse transportation. It recalled houses I had loved in England, now shaken and rattled by motor traffic. Here, vast trailers hauling 32-foot Hinckley yachts brushed by the bay window of the tiny house which sat whitely glowing in the Edward Hopperish sunlight across from an abandoned red brick sardine factory right on the Harbor, opposite its twin fishing village, Bernard.

At the time, I thought how sweet it would be to live in that tiny white house, clean and quiet. A zen-like life of simple tasks and mental clarity might be experienced there. I loved what I saw of Swan's Island, but *this* little white house glowed in my imagination. As it was now glowing in the reddish late summer light....

So, the next morning when I roused Ken out of his sleeping bag with the bright idea of my staying on alone through the winter, we returned to Bass Harbor and looked through the *Bar Harbor Times* over morning coffee in the garden of The Seafood Ketch which was about to shut down for the winter.

I marked a few telephone numbers, one in particular that advertised A Winter retreat for Artist/Writer. We hiked up the hill once more to the Swan's Island Ferry station where there was a pay telephone and tried all the numbers. The only one that answered turned out to be the people who owned the little white house I admired. Of all the houses that stand empty in need of a renter or house sitter on Mount Desert Island in the winter, it was this one, just a few hundred yards down the road from the Ferry which was the most perfect. After meeting with the owners who live next door, and further consideration over another cup of coffee (and a vile local concoction of fried dough called a Poorboy) I decided to take it. This was no simple choice. It meant being alone for months in an isolated spot, a way of life I had periodically chosen in the past, in Ireland and in England; it meant returning temporarily to New York to quit my teaching job at Cooper Union, a job I rather liked, and preparing my apartment for someone to look after it while I was away; and returning also to take care of more details of my recently deceased ex-husband's estate, that is, doing his taxes, placating his relatives. It meant clearing the decks, taking a chance, breaking the then-pattern of my life.

Or was I reinforcing a more comprehensive pattern? After all, I had "bolted" before. In June of 1972, I had gone to Ireland for a James Joyce Symposium and, still in the midst of graduate school in Ohio and with my eight-year-old son accompanying me, had gone on to Zurich then Wales then Oxford and--in keeping with a dream I had had about getting a job with Oxford University Press--had walked into the Press, got the job, put my son in school, and so a summer scholar's holiday triggered by James Joyce interests in Dublin (I gave my first academic paper at the Symposium) and Zurich (visited friends and my Joyce mentor) turned into a seven-year sojourn. I was young. I burnt bridges, I took uncalculated risks, suffered anxiety, caused my son some distress as well as fun. I had adventures, then returned to Ohio in 1980 (to a temporary job as editor at *The Kenyon Review*) with an Oxford degree, two books in progress, and debts and riches not yet fully assessed.

But my Ireland/Zurich/Wales/Oxford/London/Italy days remain a part of the watery ways of my life: the Liffey, the Limmatt, the Avon, the Isis, the Cherwell, the Thames, the Shannon, the Olentangy, the Hudson; the English Channel, the Irish Sea...the Atlantic Ocean.

To me, the word *Maine* means the sound of water. Fresh water compressed from pink granite and running down the pebbly mossy shore, through the miniature worlds of tidal pools, into the tempestuous sea. I hear the bluey-greeny-grey sea water beating an irregular rhythm against the hull of a boat nosing determinedly into the waves; water rolling and withdrawing, beating and pulling interminably at the ever-changing shingled shore. I hear Mathew Arnold's "long withdrawing roar" of his poem *Dover Beach.*

There is a rhythm in the lapping of water, but the scope of its implicit pattern is beyond our comprehension. There is a pattern in the feeding habits of birds who respond to the rhythms of the high and low tides-- opportunism of Nature's wealth and part of the grand cycle of self-renewal. It is that Pattern into which the kayak paddler yearns to enter as naturally as a bird or fish or seal, and yet is not able fully to participate at the unconscious innocent plane of, say, the Wordsworthian child who is yet "trailing clouds of glory" from a previous heavenly home. Intimations of reincarnation, perhaps, Mr. Wordsworth?

The paddler is still the conscious observer of that naturally ordered environment into which he or she yearns to be taken, to be at one with It. Kept apart by the comforting thoughts of the picnic fare tucked away in the drybags along with the necessary marine paraphernalia. Oh, but if we could swoop down from the blue to scoop up a fish with our hooked feet from the surface of the sea, dive like a gannet or a gull, become an osprey or an eagle!

But we are sea-kayakers. We wait. We place ourselves. We have listened to the marine radio, read again the tide charts. We have planned, ever so carefully, to feel as free as possible, mindful of the Oneness and all the while aware that the thinnest of skins--rubber-covered canvas stretched over a collapsible skeleton--holds us as in the palm of a hand as we rest upon, or battle with, the icy water that would kill us if we were immersed for more than a few minutes. Therein, too, perhaps, lies part of the attraction. To become something like a wild creature, which our planning paradoxically allows us to do, yet knowing that the challenge to survival that Nature poses to our species as to no other is inseparably a part of this endeavor. To lose consciousness of our individual human involvements and struggles in the world, the constructed world which we must by nature have, for it comes out of our imperfect being, and at the same time to heighten consciousness on the brink of transcending it--and to know our own being in the present moment. To emulate the concentration and grace of the Great Blue Heron fishing, his going-on-being-fishing is Pure Zen.

Ken & Author, Swan's Island Lighthouse. Photo: Ken Wade

SINGING TO SEALS, SAILING WITH DOLPHINS

No need talk of the long sunny days when the temperature was 30 below and the snow piled against the door, nor of my beautiful woodpile that took on a new diminished configuration every day; no need to talk of the lonely morning walks at "my own" little pebbly beach down behind Hinkley's boatyard where I scavenged or sat looking out to sea listening to the endless beating of wave against stone; no need to talk of the days walking in the pine forests, of sitting at the foot of the cliff under the lighthouse and contemplating the buffleheads and gannets who bobbed fishing on the gelatinous winter waves; no need to speak of my discovery of the world of tidal pools at Sea Wall, of miniature Zen gardens that sprang up spontaneously in Acadia. Of the nights sitting alone with my fiddle or a book and stoking the big wood stove while the little old house was shaken by winter storm. Of the countless expeditions with real estate agents to inspect damp drafty picturesque farmhouses that had been for sale for years…. Of the dream of permanent solitude punctuated with occasional ten-hour drives down to New York City, my Jeep laden with boxes of live lobsters for Ken and neighbors… I made it through the winter. I finished the final galley proofs of my book on Yeats. And learned what I had already known in England and Ireland--that too much beauty unshared will break your heart.

Very early the following spring, in May of 1991, Ken and I went out at dawn on one of our day-long expeditions. In the little white house at Bass Harbor the bedroom at the top of the stairs has three long skylights like glazed arrow slits; they let in the earliest morning light from the pre-dawn "rush hour" traffic, the few trucks and cars off the Swan's Island Ferry beaming their headlights in the dark on their way to work in Ellsworth or Bar Harbor. Yet it was not easy to wake up and get on our feet in the chilly air. The wood stove downstairs had burnt out during the night. We intended to carry out Ken's plan to get to Gott's Island just as the dawn sunlight broke over the horizon.

As the little house trembled to the vibrations of the traffic which passed only twelve inches from its little front door, and streaks of yellow light fanned across the rafters, we looked at each other with silent determination, dumped the cats off the foot of the bed and followed them down to the kitchen. We looked forward to a warm sunny day at sea. By the time we'd had our coffee, fixed the picnic, packed all the gear into the boat, and dressed in cold-water gear, a pink dawn lit the red brick of the abandoned sardine factory.

We carry Ken's Klepper down the short steep hill to the gravelly ramp by Rich's pungent pile of lobster traps. We have a Plan--to reach the mussel beds at Gott's and Placentia Islands and gather enough for a really big seafood pasta supper we would consume with a bottle of local wine: Coastal Red. I took along a couple of string bags.

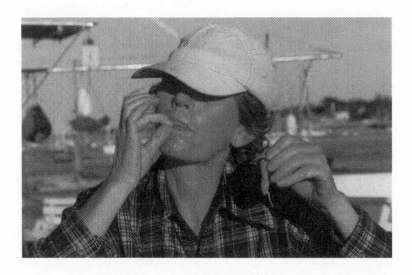

Southwest Harbor, Maine. First Lobster 9/90. Photo: Ken Wade

At this time of the morning when the air above the water and the land reaches an equal temperature the surface of the water is like lavender satin. We paddle out of the still misty harbor with the tide. A white lobster boat with a pea-green cabin revs its diesel engine and churns past us on the pinky blue water, its wake fanning out across the silky surface is rocking us gently. We turn the prow of the red Klepper into the frothy wavelets that dissolve behind us into the morning calm to join the relentless wash against the pink granite foot of Bass Harbor Head lighthouse glowing white above the dark pointed firs and the pale blue and yellow horizon.

It is important to avoid rounding Harbor Head where two currents meet in a perpetual turbulence, even now beneath the apparent mirror-calm surface of the Harbor. There is a buoy moored there that rings a deepthroated bell at every bob and surge. Many people on the island have wind chimes hanging by their back doors, chimes that mimic the tones of various bell-buoys around the island. Just as some towns or city neighborhoods have characteristic church bells, MDI rings with, and is ringed by, bell-buoys that ring, sounding not to a man-made schedule of hours for prayer, but according to Nature's patterns in a continual and erratic reminder of the need for mindfulness of the dangers from the suddenly shifting sea. Like the stories of myths that create virtual worlds of possible realities, the buoys hint at other events, past and probable, which, under other conditions--a change of season, a turn in the weather--provide occasion for drama, sudden action and frantic reaction.

We avoid the choppy water where two currents meet and paddle out across the mouth of the Harbor to skirt the ocean side of Gott's Island. What god lives there now? I wonder. As the roar of the lobster boat subsides, seals' heads begin to bob up to have a look at us. From beneath the water, from the seal's perspective (as some girl told me once in a chance conversation at Seawall) the outline of a kayak and the shadow cast by the paddler looks like a shark. What do they make of a double kayak that casts an image above them of a shark-shape with *two* dorsal fins? What do they think?

Ken says: "Seals don't think."

Ah, okay. Just to look without wanting to prove anything. This thought reminds me once again to get simple, stop the "chatter in the mind," as the Gurdieff people say, as the Zen practice says: become empty, keep an unbiased mind. I had been spending time with these disciplines while making art the summer of '89 before Ken and I met... and began the life of getting out of town, out of the library, and on the water.

The ocean side shore of Gott's is constructed of immense slabs of pink granite thrown into dolmen structures by centuries of wind and surf, shaping and reshaping the coastlines of innumerable islands each, like snowflakes, unique and yet the same. Infinite variations on a theme: Deep blue-grey-green water, white foam, pink slabs and boulders rimmed by dark green-black pointed firs clinging to the thin topsoil and outlined against the brilliant blue. What we project onto the scene; our irrepressible desire for "history" and for "meaning" is put to shame by the pure indifferent self sufficiency of this seascape, the ancient archipelago of the Gulf of Maine.

Out to our left, the open ocean; to our right, the shore where waves beat and foam and withdraw and rush in again in their Sisyphean task. Now that the sun has risen, the air temperatures of land and water have lost their equilibrium, that balance which lets the water get calm. A breeze is whipping the surface water toward shore, and us with it, while the outgoing tide pulls beneath in the opposite direction.

ALISON ARMSTRONG

We turn the kayak to head toward a gap in the island and hope there will still be enough water to get through the passage that, at low tide, reveals immense beds of mussels. I raise the gib by ropes and pulleys without losing my seat in (a system we'd worked out in quiet swampy lagoons in Adirondack lakes) and we catch the wind that carries us between two leaning towers of bright granite. Ken guides us through with the rudder.

One slab slopes down into the water, a smooth natural ramp like the floor of some ruined cathedral. We edge up to it sideways and disembark to stretch our legs on the giant stones. We are beginning to feel hot in our layers of cold-water gear: "combinations" or long johns of polypropylene covered by dry-suits, I wear "farmer john" type bib overalls with neoprene at the ankle closings and a matching windbreaker with a silk turtleneck shirt underneath, and socks and high rubber boots. I've already got a strip of sunburn around each ankle where I pulled up my trousers above my boot tops. We have not yet discovered neoprene wet boots which, like a wetsuit, retain water next to the skin that keeps it at body temperature -- theoretically -- after the initial shock of the cold plunge as you wade into the water to enter the kayak. And they help you keep your footing if you must disembark on a rough pebbly shore. The ocean still held -- as indeed it does all year -- more than a suggestion of winter's cold. Even in the height of summer's heat Maine waters are cold enough to kill you.

If you are suddenly immersed after being capsized, you can die of cold-shock in the water, or, later, of hypothermia. The sudden shock of cold water surrounding an unprotected body can cause the heart-rate to accelerate, induce uncontrollable shaking and panting which increases the likelihood of taking in water through the mouth and nose; the inability to hang on to a rope or to the side of the kayak because the hands lose all feeling. Nerve control goes, or, in the more gradual process of hypothermia, the core body temperature drops below a point that can be regained and, even after rescue men who have been immersed for twenty minutes or more have died even after being rescued, wrapped in dry blankets, and given a hot drink. So when the sun is hot and the sky is clear and one is tempted to jump into a kayak in only a T-shirt and swimsuit, it seems against reason to bundle up.

You may be starting off from shore in 80-degree weather, yet after passing the last point of land, you feel the air temperature drop significantly and despite the warm rays of the sun and the desire for an even tan, you are glad of the extra clothing...until you approach the sunbaked granite shore.

Although I enjoy having the "correct gear" for all sporting activities, I often wish that I were a seal, with all the insulation snugly contained beneath a sleek waterproof skin: no toggles, no zippers, no pockets, no odds and ends to think of: acquadynamic.

We re-entered the kayak from our pink-sugar ledge of granite, after stretching our legs and removing a layer of inner clothing, and made our way through the shallows between Gott's and Placentia.

We had been paddling on the ocean side for several hours and now the sun was high and bright blue water was dancing up and down in shivery little peaks where the retreating tides were whipped by a breeze. At low tide we gathered as many purple-shelled mussels as our string bags would hold and attached them to D-rings on the side of the kayak to drag in the cold water and keep fresh until dinner time. Gathering mussels is as easy as picking grapes, unlike clamming which is hard backbreaking work; you must bend over with fork in hand chasing the bubbles of panting clams as they race beneath the soggy sand in desperate and clever attempts to elude you.

Mussels, they almost invite you to pluck them from their pebbly bed; it is important not to tear their "beards" with which they cling to the stones, for if you take their "anchors," they stay fresh and alive, perhaps not realizing that they are being transported along with a few pebbles, from their seashore community to your kitchen. I like to keep them -- and the lobsters, too -- happy and unaware as long as possible.

We set out again towards open water, skirting tiny islands to the southeast. The wind had picked up and the surf around every rocky shore, even the gently sloping ones, was getting fierce. We passed through a maze of partly submerged rocks and saw that a large colony of seals surrounded us. We had read about them diving in fear, and abandoning their young, at the sight of a kayak. But we saw no nursing mothers with young; these fellows were so curious that they paddled furiously with their little flippers to stay in one place and lift their bodies head and shoulders above the water to get a good look at us. They seemed to be smiling. Ken began to sing an old Scottish ballad, "I am a Silky on the Sea." A Silky, or Selchie, is a seal lover who comes from the sea, takes on a human form and marries a human, then disappears back into the sea. At the end of a year and a day, as some tales have it, he comes back to her and demands their young son whom he takes back with him to the sea, leaving her with a sack of gold for her nurse's fee. Or, as this particular ballad says, the selchie predicts that she will marry a good gunner whose first shot will kill both his young son and himself.

The rhythm of the song was the same as the rhythm of our paddling, and the seals followed us, closer and closer. "I am a man upon the land/I am a Silky on the Sea...." They seemed hypnotized. Seals of all sizes came closer and stared right at us. Then Ken took his "boat harmonica" from the side pocket and played a rousing version of the Appalachian gospel, "Jesus on the Mainline," which involves some train imitations with plenty of vigorous sucking and blowing to get the right sound effects. All seals immediately turned up their flippers and dove.

When we resumed singing the Scots ballad, the Silky's sad rhythmic song brought them all back to surround us -- our most attentive audience in Maine, we decided later after giving a number of performances in the church and in pubs at Bar Harbor...and in the front parlor of the Victorian house at the top of Bass Harbor we were to rent the following summer...and where I would again stay on alone. But for now, we were happy, enchanted and alone on the sea with our seal audience.

Since then, in 1996, I was given a wonderful book, *The People of the Sea*, stories about seals collected by David Thomson, first published in Scotland in 1954. The final chapter, "The Music of the Seals," give examples of several songs, including "The Grey Selchie of Sule Skerrie" (similar to the ballad Ken and I sang) as well as fishermen's songs for attracting seals and songs purported to be collected from singing seals. He speculates that the oldest songs of the coastal people of Scotland and Ireland were perhaps taken from sounds made by the seals.

We paddled further out to sea and put in at a treacherous stony and windy beach on a tiny island to eat lunch. I always pack tins of sardines; Ken had made us a lovely shrimp salad, as usual. But there was no shelter from the wind, and the waves were battering our kayak onto the stones. The sunlight took on the orangey redness typical of a Maine afternoon; we repacked and with difficulty turned the Klepper back toward Bass Harbor.

We passed the seal colony's rocks and saw that they were nearly submerged in the rising tide; only a few young seals popped up to follow us through the miniature archipelago of their haul-outs. The water became glassy calm and lavender; we had the gib up but by now there was no wind. Then I heard a deep wheezing sound, a slow rasping inhalation and a sudden long drawn-out whooshing exhalation… dolphins surfacing for air and making shallow curve-backed dives. They were moving into calm protected waters surrounded by small islands. I cautiously reached forward and pulled the gib taught so that it wouldn't flap and frighten them in their play. We moved stealthily lifting our paddles in slow motion until we were in the midst of their game, their sunset dance. We sat still, becalmed and entranced on the silky evening water, out of time, as the dolphins danced around us. The spell was broken by a late-homing lobster boat's diesel engine; as the roar drowned the music of their breathing, they moved further out to sea, and we lifted our paddles reluctantly to head home to a late supper of fresh mussels, careful to avoid the Swan's Island ferry as it crossed our path coming into Bass Harbor.

HEADING INTO THE WIND, MEETING THE WAVE

When riding a horse cross country over jumps, you don't concentrate on the fast-approaching hurdle and you certainly don't look down at it as you fly over. You keep your head up, your hands steady, your legs firmly pressing your horse into the bit, your heels down. Your joints are springs for your forward-moving weight; your limbs the confidence and joy within which your horse collects and extends his body. Look beyond and you "throw your heart over the fence" which is already imagined, already accomplished.

When you paddle your kayak in wind and choppy waves, whether relentless or gusting, you head your prow into the source, the wind. Wind makes waves. Just as you work with the horse's strength and speed, so you work with/against the wind and wave patterns, which may be mild or violent, which may save you or destroy you. Divine indifference. That is, when we are suitably humble and prepared, then, like a god inviting us to some divine feast at which cruel jokes may at times be played, we are suffered to enter the magic realms.

We fancy that we can "make meaningful contact" with other creatures because we observe they are somewhat like us; yet they are *other*, creatures better provided for within their own well-defined patterns of being. They look at us with apparent indifference, fear or curiosity -- feelings with which we identify. We too eat, sleep, breed, age, endure, and die; we too behold them with curiosity, fear or indifference. But not with their innocence.

So, the wind shifts; turn your prow into it before you take in more water, another big wave like that in your lap and you'll have to bail out the extra weight and you need both hands on the paddle and both feet on the rudder pedals to maintain your tracking.

Too late now to put on the spray skirt, too late to adjust the weight of your gear where you can't reach it, up under the deck. Now turn for shore, there where the grey surf crashes against that low ledge of pink granite, a natural put-in but it is very narrow; miss it and you lose the lea side of this little island and risk capsizing if you go beyond. Prepare to turn, use your inside paddle blade as a bird uses its wing, as you would press down your heel turning your horse to flex his body around that leg; brace against the waves pounding at you before they flip you sidewise; lean into them.

If they are strong, you are cunning; if they are threatening, you are subtle and quick. And always calm. Use the elements to your advantage just as they you find them. You are traveling. Ride your boat as you ride your wind horse, your Shambala, steed of the spiritual warrior who incorporates the powers of the elements for his own salvation.

To "paddle your own canoe," an Irish song says, is to learn more about the self in relation to the higher Self. I once asked my friend Ken, who introduced me to sea kayaking, what he most liked about it. His reply: "Not having to talk to anyone." This, despite the fact that he had bought a *double* Klepper as his first boat before we met, the front seat of which I was to be assigned. Eventually, during our second summer of kayaking in Maine, he bought a marine battery for the 10-horsepower electric outboard motor that he rigged up to a wooden crossbar behind his seat in the rear of the cockpit; this battery, trailing its wires, rested between my knees on the narrow wooden floorboard.

This, along with the additional sailing gear with which he was perpetually experimenting, decided me, in the summer of '91; it was time I had my own, single, kayak. After months of looking and thinking, the summer faded, but I finally settled on a single expedition model folding sea-kayak manufactured in Vancouver. It was designed with the Inuit baidarka (skin covering a flexible lashed frame) as a model; but unlike Ken's beamy heavy German kayak with a wide open cockpit and wooden frame, mine has a high-tech aluminum frame and synthetic canvas deck. And it is not for sailing, nor for "Eskimo rolls" like the hardbodies. I decided, with my love of wooden boats unabated, that if I were going to paddle, I would paddle unencumbered; if I were going to sail, then I would sail in a wooden sailboat. (And from time to time I do, as I have two friends with vintage wooden boats.)

My great dream of horse and sailboat was still to be realized. Yet the simplicity and quiet of this graceful clean-lined kayak was irresistible; it meant a kind of freedom and closeness to nature that could not be achieved in any other way. The bright blue Feathercraft arrived in mid-winter, while I was visiting my family in Ohio. I transported it, still boxed, from the mid-west back to New York City and then back to Maine where, in late March, I would begin a teaching job at The College of the Atlantic for spring semester. But the winter weather lasted until mid-May.

However, with the help of neighbor Forrest, a kayak aficionado, we put my new boat together early in April while the snow was still on the ground. Its sixteen-plus feet took up much of the large back-parlor of my ten-room rented Victorian house at the top of the harbor. I was at least able to sit in it (along with my curious cats) while I warmed the room with the large Danish wood stove and awaited the arrival of my new Nimbus paddle. Everything, including this paddle, could (in theory) be broken down and fitted into one large canvas backpack weighing under 50 pounds which I can barely carry without putting my lower back out of commission. My kayak, unlike Ken's Klepper, is *very* tightly fitted, and I was to discover that it is nearly impossible to dismantle or reassemble it in less than a day. Still, what a terrific *idea*, to be able to get on an airplane with my boat and, someday, take it to Ireland or England or Denmark or France... But it has known only the salty waters off the coast of Maine and the brackish waters of the Hudson River. I'll get another, smaller one with a wood frame, for any future transatlantic kayak trips. It will be a Hudson River boat from now on.

When my teaching duties and the cold weather abated and I could sit out down by the shore, I took to reading about Vikings and so I named my bright new boat, which was tethered near me awaiting the tide to come in, Skidbladther, a magical mythic (or perhaps not) boat that the Norse god Frey counted among his greatest treasures. It was built by dwarves. According to Magnus Magnussen who quotes Snorri Sturluson, who wrote in the 13th century, it always had a following wind, and it was so ingeniously constructed that it was large enough to carry the whole pantheon of the gods of Asgarth. And yet it could be folded up into a bag when not being used.

Anyhow, not having to talk to anyone is often a desirable situation. From time to time I have taken a Vow of Silence, which has interesting effects. I got the idea from a weekend spent in the summer of 1989 at a Zen retreat. While I was preparing to face what had become the ordeal of completing my dissertation in comparative literature and mourning the loss of the child and yearning to be something else, somewhere else, I set aside two months to be a visual artist. I began to construct sculptures, imaginary Japanese gardens, miniature Zen environments that reproduced images from my dreams. After a couple of months of this activity, I discovered that there was a Zen Mountain Monastery near Woodstock where I had spent some happy times in the mid-60s and met my tall Poet friend, of whom more in a moment.

THE VORTEX

One hot sunny Friday in the city in 1989, I suddenly decided to catch the bus at Port Authority and go up for their week-end introductory session. The bus ride reminded me of a previous bus trip in 1966 when I had taken a Trailways from Columbus, Ohio, with my two-and-a half-year-old son; after the tedious twelve-hour ride (the longest trip I had ever taken by myself), I was met at the Village Green in Woodstock by artist friends, Isabel and Bob, who were running an Artists' Commune they called "212". They had an old property on Route 212 between Saugerties and Woodstock, several acres which included a lake they called "Mount Olive" and a huge rambling white wooden structure of three and a half stories which had been a roadhouse of ill repute. I arrived in May with my young son and a trunk of summer clothes to find that the weather up there was still wintry. I was twenty-three, newly divorced, and having my first "adventure." The box of winter clothes that my parents hastily dispatched made the rounds by bus of all the Woodstocks in New England and finally reached me in the heat of August a few weeks before I was to leave, by way of a visit to my

Cousin Bill on the Lower East Side of Manhattan -- a slimmer, tanner, wiser young lady.

But on the last leg of that bus ride from Port Authority going to Woodstock, (where a man posing as a porter nearly made off with my trunk), there was a bearded man with a pet monkey hidden under his jacket; he too got off at the Village Green and made only a few brief appearances over the summer. I bought his 5-speed bike that was stolen from the Poet friend's station wagon later in the summer.

There were all sorts of artists at the Commune: poets -- Joel Oppenheimer visited; there were rock musicians -- The Mothers of Invention came to stay for most of the summer and practiced in an old chicken house; Bob Dylan was around from time to time; and local people, too, like Luke the Plumber, along with all sorts of painters, dancers, photographers, amateur film-makers, and a man who made sculptures from melted styrofoam. One of his pieces was of bald mannequin heads mounted on a wooden platform and splashed with psychedelic paint; it floated at will, an eerie raft, on the shallow lake he had named Mount Olive.

I discovered yoghurt and wonderful dark heavy raisin-pumpernickel bread sold by the pound in the deli on the Green next to the gallery -- both owned by the lady who wore skirts to the ground; some said she had a wooden leg.

I went skinny-dipping with "The Mothers" and about 50 others; took canoe trips down the lake and into the swamp with a young fellow named "Groovy" because that's all he said -- it was the prime slang word of the day. Taught my two and a half-year-old son that he could pee in the woods "just like the Indians did."

We all tried to keep to a fair schedule of sharing and rotating chores in proper Commune fashion, and soon the artists were complaining that all they did was fix roofs, haul water, cook, and do emergency repairs on the crumbling buildings. Nobody was getting any work done, except "The Mothers." They just ate and played music in the old chicken house; I kept an eye on them while I was outside pulling weeds and watched the mountain mists ascend in the clear early summer air of the Catskills.

By the middle of the summer, there were "Happenings" to break the tension, the most spectacular being the Garbage Dump Happening at the foot of a tall cliff where the community dumped its trash. It was ...

groovy. But I had arrived practically broke in May, and got a job down the road at a hamburger stand run by a fellow who had been in the cavalry, so he said. Bob Dylan came in for a burger and fries; when I got back to "212" one afternoon it turned out that *Holiday* magazine had come and gone, taking a spectacular color photo of everyone who happened to be around at the time leaning over the railings of the three-tiered porch of the "big house."

By mid-June I had a job beyond Bearsville in Mount Tremper at All Seasons Camp for children, teaching theatre, canoeing and horseback riding. My two and a half year old son was picked up by his grandparents (my scandalized in-laws) and taken to Canada for the annual fishing trip.

I only visited "212" on the weekends when I could spend two days and a night with my Poet friend.

The best event of all was at the end of the summer, when my job had finished, I had my pay, and on Labor Day Weekend, there was a 3-day Rock Concert called "Sound-Out" -- the genuine precursor to the more (in)famous "Woodstock" (which wasn't held at Woodstock, in fact). I camped there with my Poet friend in his station wagon; and I had a job one evening selling firewood off the back of Luke's truck; in the dark, someone handed me a fifty-cent piece and I handed him an armload of wood and, as he walked away in the dark, someone said, "Hey, you just touched Bob Dylan!"

That was September 1966.

But by late July 1989, more than twenty years later, after OSU, Oxford, after NYU, I was taking the bus again from Port Authority alone, my young son having grown up of course and now a parent himself -- my son who, at the age of twelve, had announced "I will never grow up to be a Hippie like you and your friends!" and kept his word. Now, in the hot summer of 1989, having moved from living in my painting studio to an apartment on the River, I was going to a Zen monastery near Woodstock for two days and two nights on the spur of the moment to find some serenity in the midst of my midlife spiritual and intellectual and emotional upheaval.

On both occasions, I was seeking some space in the Catskills in which to realign my emotional life; the end of an important relationship, in both instances, was the context for my distress with my own creative endeavors. In 1966, I was getting a divorce and preparing to return to college with the aim of being an English professor and a Writer one day; and in 1989, a relationship which I didn't want to end was ending, I was living apart from my 2nd husband, as I was preparing to complete my graduate student days forever to be qualified at last to become a professor. But now all I wanted was to make sculpture. Never to grade another student paper, never have to read another book of lit theory, no more structuralist critiques or reader-response theories of the Great Writers. But that is another story.

My impulse to go to this Zen retreat was rewarded. I saw what seemed to be multiple manifestations of images I had seen in my dreams, the dreams which led me to make sculptures, miniature worlds capturing the essence of the gardens, rocks, trees, rivers I yearned for so deeply in my city apartments. I learned to sit Zendo; I requested (with a silent bow) vigorous whacks on either shoulder given by a tiny Japanese nun with a big stick when I felt my detached alertness fade; I tried to "be in the moment," to release clamorous painful thoughts like wild birds, let my eyes study the grain of the wood wall, attempted without desiring it to remain simple.

The Zen people were more light-hearted than the Gurdieff group with whom I had spent two work weekends chafing under their authoritarian and humorless gaze. The Sensei John Daido Loori had tattoos from his days in the Navy. He smoked and smiled and laughed. Yet he was elegant, dignified; his appearance became more Asian during the profoundly serious ceremonies. I knew he took a child-like delight in his new red tractor, realized that he had remade himself, transcended his past without denying it.

I was silent, I watched. I appreciated the disciplined schedule, the fresh air, the green of surrounding mountains and meadows...felt I was somehow on the Right Track away from my anxiety attacks. Toward... what? Deliverance into a communion with the divine silence of Forms, the divine hum of Nature. To transform from Explainer to Maker, from Critic to Artist.

On the last day, Sunday, we all went across the road and down a short path to the Esopas River where a rocky stream flowed into the wide fast-running water. Near the bank about three feet above the river I saw a worn spot; a young nun clambered up the bank and jumped into the river and disappeared in a whirlpool.

ALISON ARMSTRONG

Others followed and came up, their shaven heads bobbing in the swift current further out in the river. I, too, climbed up the bank and looked down into a small deep pool of dark churning water and then jumped. The force of the water sucked me under and down; to resist would only keep me there, trapped beneath the surface. I relaxed and let myself swirl downward with the vortex until the pressure suddenly released its hold and I could swim freely downstream, and then surface and turn to swim against the shallow rapids and back across to the rocky shore. It was a physical non-verbal lesson in literally "going with the flow," in releasing one's Will and using the power within the given situation, to work *with* Nature. I thought of Yeats's phrase: "It is a mistake to expect the Will to do the work of the Imagination."

I now knew, in my body, what it felt like to release my Will to a greater force, to trust *that* and to survive it, with joy. This, as it turned out, was part of my preparation to survive the force of the Phantom Barge which would overpower me the following summer. I remembered the humility imprinted upon the mad 18th century poet Christopher Smart who prayed to the Lord to send him Beauty and He answered the prayers, sent Smart to dive for pearls at the bottom of the sea. "Something," as Samuel Beckett wrote, "is taking its course," beyond conscious control but springing from our desire.

To get back to my friend Ken's comment about not having to talk to anyone as a good reason for kayaking: I discovered that Maintaining a Vow of Silence in the presence of another entails humility and detachment; it means you *and* your companion think twice about your own thoughts.

Instead of making a remark that is unconsidered, say, a sarcastic retort, something a bit hurtful, unnecessary observations, a comment that befogs the air between you and him, between you and the scenery, between You and How Things Are, indeed, any form of speech that is meant to fill emptiness or to aggravate a response, you eat it. Or in Zen practice you acknowledge it and set it free like a bird to fly off. You hear yourself in your head and then it, your head, grows quiet. You are humble before the mirror of your careless thoughts. You clean out the attic of your brain.

Sharing could turn to bickering on a small craft such as a double kayak. Now, with each of us "captain" of our respective kayaks, each is responsible for his and her own destiny. Ken and I have paddled side by side, as two equals ought -- except that he is stronger and sometimes leaves me in his wake. When I was in the front seat of his double, I, as he put it, had a tendency to "babble."

After all, paddling, like the rhythmic activity of walking, frees the imagination. And, when I am talking I tend to stop paddling -- to make a point, to point to something. He, "the Commodore" in the rear seat of authority, the one who owns the boat and manipulates the rudder, says that I, "the First Mate," can't talk and crew at the same time. I, "the Bad Child," retort to him, "the Stern Parent," that we aren't in a race out here and call his attention to yet another Wonder of Nature that, of course, he has already seen and quietly noted to himself: a mother osprey teaching her terrified young to dive, a bald eagle eyeing us from a lofty blue thermal, for instance. I imagine her considering us, in our elliptical red fish-shaped kayak centered in the vortex of her appetite. Ken the Commodore says, "birds don't think." But surely they *might* see similarities, make metaphoric connections, deduce by simple syllogism -- which, after all, is the foundation of all learning. Right? After all, that she *doesn't* dive-bomb us and try to snatch us up for her dinner might be proof that she has already thought: "Hmm. It looks like a fish; it resembles a long red fish; no fish are red, this fish-shape is red, therefore this is not a fish." Right?....We paddle on in silence. I pause and turn around in my seat.

"Right?" I say.

The Commodore says: "Keep paddling."

Keep counting breaths; that is how we Zen monks sit in zendo. Right.

I silently vow to take yet another Vow of Silence and wonder how long it will be before he notices, this time. I concentrate on just looking, without trying to explain or prove or recount or imagine anything. Just to see, without consequences, what IS -- the color/texture/sound/feel of the bluey-pink viscous murmuring coldness of the ocean at dawn, the dieselroar of lobster boats with green-red-blue-&-white cabins setting out for their traps beyond Harbor Head Light, beyond Gott's Island and Placentia where bobbing markers may be mistaken, by me, for the curious noses of watchful seals. It is May of 1991. It is August 1992.

Companionship. Solitude. Both are available. You let go your Will but remain poised, Mindful. There is a shared solitude out there, and

ALISON ARMSTRONG

whether I am manning the front seat of the red double Klepper, or trailing behind in my own blue single Feathercraft, there is a quiet undercurrent of shared memory, of the good will it engenders. We would rescue one another if the occasion called for it.

Which leads me to recall how it all began in 1990, the sea kayaking. This pursuit of a "meaningless" activity, this "simply messing about in boats." I am Mole; he is Ratty. From the Hudson, a tidal river of great complexity, filth, beauty, force and danger, we traveled to quiet lakes in the Adirondacks, to Lake Champlain, then the fjord of Somes Sound and the sheltered depths of Echo Lake and Long Pond on Mount Desert Island, to the turbulent shore at Sea Wall from which I imagined we might keep paddling straight across the Atlantic until we reached the Aran Islands and Galway Bay. Setting out for the nearest island, three miles away, we are a red speck upon the deep blue swells edged with rich green spruce fringing great slabs of bright pink granite frothed by the relentless tide that would push us back to our earthbound unbuoyant merely human condition. *Meerschaum.* Our exuberance is exhausted when we reach Duck Island, badly in need of a stretch and a picnic, only to find that it is a bird sanctuary. We reembark and shove off against the pebbly shore; the water is so clear you can see down several feet to the rocks below which reflect the sun back into the air. I give a prayer of thank-you-God recalling the poem that came to me more than two years earlier: the image of sunlight on clear pebble shining through the waves of clear water, the lapping of the water like the synchronized breathing of lovers.

Seals crowd in, having seen that we are beings like themselves, detachable from our shark-shaped pod, realizing perhaps that we are not the Inuit of olden days come for their fur and blubber. The water is so cold our ankles ache long after we've have launched off the rocky shore against wind and wave and eased our bottoms into the small seats below the level of the surface of the sea.

When the tide turns and runs out away from all the edges of the islands, the level of the ocean seems higher than that of the shore. Where does all that water go, after all, when it is pulling apart from the land as if drawn by an invisible magnet?

Does it, like fire, aspire to the heavens? Does it *feel* the pull of the moon? From where I sit, it feels to me as though it is doing two things at once: *beneath* the surface it is leaving the land in a steady sucking force, while *on* the surface the wind is pushing the waves to roll onwards towards the shore. Live water and live land, contending for the upper hand, to parody T.S. Eliot's wasted image. Therefore, you feel in the seat of your pants the surface of the water urging your boat on towards shore with the help of a following wind, yet at the same time you feel in the blades of your two-ended paddle the tug and pull backwards of the outrushing waters.

This was the case when we encircled what we thought was Little Cranberry Island, saw what seemed to be immense islands slowly moving across the horizon toward Great Cranberry and finally realized that these were huge swells coming in from the ocean toward The Gut. We swung out away from the granite shore to allow time and space in which to maneuver so that we would have both wind and water at our backs before being wrecked sideways upon the rocks.

It was a roller coaster ride in slow motion, once we got our prow headed for the opening in the land and the giant whale-humps of swelling water carried us in long thrusts into the Gut; the surface of the water, which had seemed smooth from a distance, now showed that up-and-down choppiness characteristic (as I was learning) of the conflicting forces of wind and tide. A concerned lobsterman pulled his boat near; at first we were alarmed by the noise of his engine, being all too aware of the dangers of motorized craft due to our near death experience the month before on the Hudson River.

However, he was genuinely concerned about our rapid passage through this rough watery opening in the island which, he warned, was full of "wicked big" submerged rocks. Our task was to keep our prow directly in line with the following wind and keep up our strong steady paddling, never mind aching joints and sore backs. The large rudder, which Ken controls with foot pedals, steadied us. We had no keel to worry about, of course, and with the rubberized, rather than wooden, hull we were more likely to be bounced and flipped over than crushed if we should strike a stone.

We were paddling with the gib sail up that day, which gave us extra speed, and our ride through The Gut into the serene lagoon of Great Cranberry resembled a ride on a bucking bronco.

After a brief rest at the safe haven of The Pool, we tried to make our way across the harbor to Manset only to find ourselves in the midst of a regatta of rather large Hinckley yachts in Southwest Harbor. The pistol shots of the starters did not, however, distress a silvery-grey adolescent seal who accompanied us to the put-in where we had stashed a bike.

I cycled back to Sea Wall to get the car while Ken partially dismantled the kayak and stowed the sail and mast in their bags. As I pedalled along the country roads, it struck me that we, who had known one another for less than four months, might end up perishing together before we'd really got to know each other. At this stage, August 1990, we had mainly been "messing about" with Ken's boat. And I was learning to play the fiddle that he had given me so that we could perform together. He was very nurturing and encouraging of me with the music, teaching me his repertoire. John Jackson, John Prine. I took to it like a duck to water.

We practiced in the woods. I was letting go, relaxing my grip on all those endeavors and ambitions that had kept me tied to a desk, locked in a library grading papers, living in my head -- and others' heads, only. Boats, water, weather, music, and good food were our only concerns now.

A frustrated academic yearning for the world of speechless things, I had, the previous summer before meeting Ken, begun to make non-verbal constructions, miniature environments for my soul, places of silence. My workshop was my small apartment overlooking the Hudson. This began two years earlier with a dream while I was sleeping in my studio. My brain was over-full of Lit. Crit., Lit. Theory.

But out of some deep calm source, I'd had a visionary dream, had captured that vision in a poem, and finally set about expressing that poem-vision in a way to directly *show* it. I began to arrange water-smoothed stones and sheets of glass, to *build* the image of sunlight shining through clear water onto pebbles, to manifest it.

And here I was, a year or so later, in the natural Zen garden of the Maine coast. What happened when Ken guided me to Maine was that I discovered the manifestation of that vision/poem/sculpture in the phenomenal tangible world of Acadia. Art made magic.

The visionary image of that poem, which was translated into German, and "Japanese Impressions," became *"Eindrucke,"* that ends with the forms of pebbles illuminated by sunshine piercing the lap-lapping inspiration and exhalation, the breathing, of water which is like the breathing of two lovers lying together. I had piles of white water-rounded quartz pebbles picked up in Ireland and on Long Island shores at Northport and Amagansett, and I found a sheet of plywood which had a birch grain that resembled both the pattern of waves and the pattern impressed or imprinted (be*eindruckt*) by wavelets on the sand; I got several sheets of plate glass the same size as the plywood sheet (approximately two feet by three feet). I stacked the sheets of glass upon layers of stone. I wanted to see how many layers I could make and still keep the "impression" of my dream image: *Gestalten unserer Kinder.*

Describing this recalls an earlier dream I had had during my first term as graduate student at NYU, a terrifying dream that illustrated for me my deep ambivalence about the "cathedral of learning" that is the university. In this great stone dream cathedral was suspended a floor of glass high above the stones of the aisle below--metaphor for the illusion and impermanence of language, of literary theory. (We were reading Derrida's *GLAS* in white-bearded Geoffrey Hartman's seminar at the time.) So long as I *believed he was supported*, the white-bearded be-robed figure of The Wise Man would remain (naively, I felt) held up by the platform of glass high above the stone floor.

But when I doubted I became a bat darting about under the vaulted arches, the glass shattered, and I was brutally swept down a set of collapsing wooden stairs onto the cold stone, and Satan stepped forward (in traditional red and black, with cape, horns and a pointed tail!) and handed me a KitKat candy bar as a "consolation prize." (In Hartman's seminar, we were also reading the religious poetry of Christopher--Kit Smart.)

That was in the autumn of 1982. Now, in 1989, I was approaching the end of that long struggle of academic work and lonely sacrifice and feeling like a trapped mule plodding after an ever-withering carrot at the end of an ever-lengthening stick.

I could not eat, I could not read. I wanted only the silence of sculpture. Pure form. With a feeling of vindication, I listened when my friend Richard, a sculptor with literary interests told me that he liked Samuel Beckett's saying that his task as a writer was "to restore things to their silence." This friend was once an anthropologist who had given up academia twenty years earlier. He began to abhor his scholarly intrusions into the sanctity of the lives of his "subjects" in a Mexican village. He saw that he could change space by juxtaposing two sticks in Central Park; he went to Spain, he went to Paris. He became a sculptor, an earth mover. He concern is gravity, silence, to perpetually make the world strange again. To restore it to awe.

I had other "silenced" images in my head in addition to my pebbles under clear lapping water lit by sunlight, images from other dreams, good dreams of beckoning tree tops, of simple huts. . .and from Yeats's poetry: "...like a long-legged fly/her mind moves upon silence." It seems that the coast of Maine was already embedded in my spirit and only awaited my arrival which was really a return. A manifestation of a mental state.

Exactly one month after I had bought my Inner Child her red and white wooden sailboat with real cloth sails, I met Ken. He was to become a friend by introducing me to sea kayaking in his double German Klepper, with a red canvas deck stretched on a wooden frame, and soon with sails. He had seen two of my Japanese-Zen-garden dream inspired constructions that had been exhibited in a group show at the gallery in our building that autumn of 1989, the end of my transformative year when, within one incredible week of intense focus of energy, I had successfully revised and defended my Ph.D. dissertation. While I was renovating my apartment with my German sculptor friend the telephone rang; someone wanted to buy the larger construction; could he come by that night a put a deposit on it? Of course. I felt I was on a roll, the hard times were over at last it seemed. I spent the money from that first sale of my sculpture on a car trip to Vermont and we brought back stones.

Ken had inquired about my work at the gallery during that show, but he didn't say anything to me about it until the following April, one sunny afternoon, when I was coming out of my apartment door. A man in a baseball cap stopped me and said: "were those your wood sculptures I liked so much in the gallery last fall?" "I hope so," I replied.

He said he'd like to see more of my work. I said that my door was open and he could come in right now and have a look at my work. I had seen him, a trim redheaded man about my height wearing a baseball cap, going in and out of our building for years quietly walking his golden retriever, and once he brushed past me like a shadow at a gallery opening in SoHo. But now he held up his hands, covered in black grease and replied, "Some other time, I'm working on my car." That old car, as it turned out, would take the two of us to Acadia.

A couple of nights later, at sunset, I was leaving the building by the riverside door with my bicycle to go to dinner in TriBeCa with some friends. He of the baseball cap was just coming into the building with his bicycle. We stopped to disentangle our bikes, talked about the sunset over the Hudson, and did I want to go for a bike ride together? Now? No. Soon? Did I like boats? I mentioned my new toy wooden sailboat. He said he had just bought a red double folding kayak -- not one of those plastic hard-bodied jobs--and he wanted me to come out with him in it. I was interested. Here was Someone to Do Things With. At my friends' dinner-party an hour later I happily announced that I had just met a nice man who had asked me to become his kayak-mate. As it turned out, my anthropologist-turned-sculptor friend at this dinnertable had known Ken years ago when he was active as an artist; Ken would soon inspire him to buy his own red double German sea-kayak and, a month or so later, join him in forming the Downtown Boat Club, from which Ken and I would make a fateful launching July 3rd.

BARGE + TUG on Hudson

AA
6.29.90

*   *   *

NEWS RELEASE: July 5, 1990

Early in the morning of July 4th, shortly past midnight, Alison Armstrong and Ken Wade, while sailing on the Hudson River in the latter's seventeen-foot sea kayak, were struck from behind by the starboard prow of an unlit barge. The steel-clad barge was being propelled at approximately 15 knots by a white tug on its port stern.

Ken, Alison, and the kayak were sucked beneath the oncoming barge and remained trapped under water while the 300-foot vessel passed overhead.

Their emergency flares brought no response. Forty-five minutes later, having been carried by the outgoing current, from about 80th Street down to about 34th Street, in the middle of the river, four young men in a cabin cruiser heard their SOS whistle, saw their small remaining light, and rescued them.

They were picked up by paramedics at the Imperial Marina in Weehawken, New Jersey, who took them by ambulance to Saint Mary's Hospital in Hoboken, where they were treated for shock. Ken sustained a head wound and received stitches. Lt. Maher of the Marine Inspection Unit of the U.S. Coast Guard, and the 20th Precinct of NYPD have been notified of the collision; neither seem to know how to trace the tug pilot. After long deliberation, the police recorded the incident as a hit-and-run.

*   *   *

This press release was completely ignored by the news media. We learned, too late, from a brochure sent to us by a Lt. Maher of the Coast Guard, that "The speed of a ship, towboat, or tugboat can be deceptive. A tow can travel one mile in seven minutes--a ship even faster--and it take 3/4 to 1 1/2 miles to stop...if a water skier falls a thousand feet in front of a moving tug or tow, the skier has less than one minute to get out of the way...be aware that a tug or tow's powerful engines can cause a smaller vessel to be pulled toward the tow...."

A lengthier account of our accident, entitled "The Phantom Barge," was published the following summer in *Sea Kayaker*, a Seattle magazine. A cautionary tale, they called it. It follows this essay.

That accident, that gift of a nudge from the Beyond, that reminder of mortality, took place in the summer of 1990 at midnight, one minute into the 4th of July. Exactly twelve hours later, the following noon, my former husband died. A few days before, he and I shared a taxi uptown to his hospital for out patient treatment. He asked me to come and talk with him about getting back together. He'd said, "You keep telling me that you'll do anything if I need it. We need to have a long talk. If I could understand what went wrong in our marriage then I can get well again."

Somehow he linked his lymphoma to a failure…of what? Comprehension? Communication? Love? If he could fix our marriage, then he could fix his suffering body. That was the implication. Perhaps he could, miraculously, have recovered from the cancer, that horror which invaded his being. It was not his "fault," after all; he was haemophilic, had been given contaminated blood, the clotting-factor-8, that it had made him HIV-positive. We did not know this until the year after I had left him and moved to our studio on the floor below because I felt driven away by his incomprehensible demands that I should "shape up" and behave like other women. I had left not knowing he would become ill. I had left to pursue my own goals that he could neither accept nor understand. And so I agreed to talk whenever he wanted (he was still in the old apartment just above my new one, in Westbeth); he planned to call me in a day or two, as soon as his visiting relatives left. I never received his call, never had that long talk, never suspected that his end was so near. Good intentions, all too late.

Could I have helped him to save his life by returning? Could I have saved Philipp by walking down another street and stopping him when he was running back to Westbeth that April afternoon to throw himself from the roof? Robert tried to console me over Philipp's death; who could console me over his? Theirs? Ken did not understand grieving, he said. Besides he loathed Philipp who had lived in the next-door apartment for twenty years, that wall that separated them a constant battlement. And he didn't particularly like Robert.

Likewise, my German sculptor friend did not understand remorse. He was friendly with Philipp, as they were both German artists. And he didn't particularly like Robert. Philipp didn't particularly like Robert, either, but had played chess with him for twenty years.

I was to learn how much time they take--grief and remorse, how much energy from the demands of the living. One lives in two worlds at once, the gravity of the past tugs at the inertial on-going motion of the present; this is how one is kept in orbit…the elliptical track with two focal points, two centers of two overlapping circles, the What If and the What Now.

In addition to coping with the dismay and shock after our survival of what might well have been a fatal encounter for Ken and myself, I

ALISON ARMSTRONG

also had the shock and grief in the aftermath of Robert's death--dealing with his brother and sister and brother-in-law who returned after having just visited, taking the cats and the plants that we once had shared, distributing copies of the death certificate, emptying his apartment; I had to deal with my guilt at not being on hand when he was suddenly taken to hospital while I was out on the river. If this were fiction you would not believe it, the timing seems too contrived. And the irony: while Robert was departing this life, I might have preceded him by 12 hours, yet was given a new chance at life, life with a new perspective, a chance to free myself of old inhibitions.

The wailing and flashing of sirens which carried him (dying) to an uptown hospital on the East River and me (without a scratch) to the Hoboken hospital on the Hudson River were drowned by the garish flashing and exuberant explosions of early 4th of July celebrants.

Now (in 1993) the third summer has come and gone since that experience, that mysterious and powerful reminder that Leviathan lurks to plow under, in the midst of joy and hope, all plans and good intentions... Where am I? Who am I? Back in my Hudson River apartment in Westbeth Artist Housing, after two years spent mainly in Maine, I have lived in the manifestation of my dream-inspired sculptures, and (thanks to Robert) some new possessions: Shambala my Windhorse-Jeep with which to carry Skidbladther, my boat that can carry all the gods and yet folds up into a sack. I even have my own real life version of "Vinnie-der-Pooh," a teddybear-like part-Chow dog from the animal shelter on Mount Desert Island. The gentleman dog I suspect of being her sire, a big bully of a white Chow who had the run of Bass Harbor, terrorized my usually unflappable grey cat more than a year before my doggie was born to somebody's unsuspecting lady Skye terrier. Yes, she *is* a type of substitute child as well as living reminder of that visionary place. The day I adopted her I took her to Sea Wall and we walked among the tidal pools I love so much. I thought Romantic Thoughts such as: I stand in the sea-spray of the tumult of memories, with renewed faith in the power of the unconscious to manifest itself in the world through our creative expression.

And now, the fourth summer has come and gone since that Experience; after a year back in my New York apartment by the river and the noise of the West Side Highway, and the restlessness, the yearning to be Still, I began to come to the Hudson Highlands. Ken, who claims to be my soul mate, is a type of Loki the trickster, a type of Mercury the messenger. He had once brought me to Garrison's Landing on a November day to help our friend Rip prepare to take his old wooden sailboat out of the water; I became enchanted with the place, the mountains plunging into the River-fjord. I began to go up every weekend to sell my antiques, I met a former Westbeth resident who found me a job with Outward Bound (my office had a view of the River), she found me a cabin to rent, I met others who had moved here, one who had been my husband Robert's architecture student, another a writer who had crossed my path years earlier in Ireland and New York--and soon I was living here most of the time, again, as the result of my mental images and sculptures of rocks and water, my ink sketches of huts in a forest surrounded by mountains. What I made became what I did; what I imagined became my new reality.

To look, to kayak, to be with mute animals who show me unconditional love...I stay alone, get quiet, in between part-time jobs with congenial friends. Solitude. And then the Writing, the Making, comes. More slowly, more tentatively, than it did in the City when creating a quiet haven in the mind was a defense against outer turmoil, noise, dirt, and danger. Order seeks itself, too, out of the Chaos of past impressions and emotion, of hopes fulfilled and expectations demolished, of false objects of desire.

Yeats wrote: "Ireland hurt me into poetry." So are we all "hurt" into art which gives back its own joy, companionship, emotion in the open-ended making of it. In the pushing back the wall of the not-yet, in moving into the cloud of unknowing which parts as we move into it. In filling the emptiness of the unforeseeable.

The open water shimmers in the light of the setting sun. We often sit by the Hudson and watch. You can see the tide moving incredibly fast in the middle of the river; when the tide shifts the water can be going up in the middle and down along the banks; or dead flat at slack tide, when the wind is still.

The river has its complex patterns confined within its banks, in places a fjord as at Storm King Mountain near where I also live, now. The androgynous River, "Ole Man Ribber," or Grande Dame, or Indifferent Force subject to other forces of indifferent patterns -- seems alive.

And what is a life? What is alive? Whatever moves and feels--or is perceived to move and feel, is mutable. Even the apparent permanence

ALISON ARMSTRONG

of stones, "the bones of the earth," even rocks that press upward through the living soil, they give us footing, they tower above the water where two elements meet, yet even stone is mutable, vulnerable. The vertical Palisades have mates on the coast of Africa from whom the living breathing ball of the Earth and the rising of the undulating Ocean has separated them. One's heart goes out to the stones as to any mortal creature even as they--objects of our meditation--give us our strength of spirit. Even they, like us, will not remain the same forever. And yet we find a sense of immutable selfhood in the surrender to simple awareness, acceptance of being in the moment, unquestioning, uncomplicated by emotion. The peace and fullness of being Still is the gift of the Zen Mountain Monastery.

And why should all that we see have life and not those men whom I have loved and who have died? Why should this green cricket chirp or that white moth breed and fly into my lamp and be alive when those I have known are no more? In fear and grief we cling to the Once-was and weep for the mortality of the earth and our own part in it...for those in it we held in our lives and loved *as* we knew them. We resist such change with anger and grief when it impresses itself into our existences, our illusory sense of self and cravings for stability. I tell myself a story and let it go. Robert and Philipp, those casualties of Westbeth, are sitting now and forever on some cloud playing chess as they used to do; David makes his poems and waits for me beneath every reflecting pool.... Farewell. And Patric Farrell, the "professional Irishman", and impresario, at eighty-four, dying in his Celtic frenzy, to join his beloved Elsa.

If the task of the artist is to make order from chaos, useful culture out of unruly Nature, to create the illusion of stability, *stasis,* a momentary experience of wholeness and stillness in the midst of the relentless tidal effluvia of experience, then one needs a long life, or to act quickly. Even works of art succumb to the mutability of others' "interpretations" as well as physical decay. Even ephemeral language, in many ways the most durable material of all the arts, cannot fix a moment for all time for that, too, is subject to mis-prision, that is, interpretation--and the impossibilities of direct translation. Our restless eyes look at the world and see what is within. Our eyes must be taught to rest on the form of what Is. To trust the Stillness, to trust Things as They Are. Just look, just paddle, just breathe.

It seems that we have the power to imagine, and what we imagine has the power to manifest itself.

During the summer of 1987, when we were in Venice for a Joyce-Vico conference, I had an idea for saving Venice from sinking. With my husband Robert, an architectural historian, as my "editor," I imagined a section of a novella in which a young man and an old woman in a gondola in Venice are struck by an ocean liner in the Grand Canal; the woman suffers a stroke which renders her speechless and, thus *silenced*, she reexamines her past life; the man is struck in the head, decapitated. While the consequences of what would later happen on the Hudson River in 1990 to Ken and me were far less drastic, our own "accident" seems, in retrospect, foreshadowed by my fiction, written before we met.

One late afternoon, a week before Ken and I set sail on that fateful trip up the Hudson, I was sitting on Pier 26 alone with a sketch pad. I drew a barge being pushed down river by a tugboat. I thought it looked beautiful against the sunset. I was waiting for Ken who had taken off for the weekend as a result of an argument. I discovered that he had forgotten to take some of the crucial parts of his kayak with him, which leant some amusement to my otherwise lonesome heart. He returned, somewhat abashed, and we agreed to go on the river the the next day.

Our afternoon sail on The Day of the Barge was meant to be a reunion, a tentative attempt to patch up our friendship. While we were sailing down river and the light was waning, a few hours before the barge struck, I was telling Ken, because he insists he is Catholic, about the medieval church's notion of Satan as Leviathan, the whale who lures unsuspecting lost sailors to land on its back and rest as it floats in the black sea; only when they light a fire to warm themselves and cast a light in the darkness does the mighty monster of the deep awaken and plunge them into the depths of perdition. Thus does Satan lure and deceive. Temptation of easy salvation becomes the very Master of Doom. I was just babbling, as usual, because I was so enchanted with the mighty dignity and picturesqueness of barges and tugs, the whales of the river.

The Bestiary was used for a very different notion from today's ecologically-minded sentiments about whales, for the whale was once a metaphor for Evil, or at least the primeval forces of Chance -- what Melville did with Moby Dick, what Yeats did with the Great Herne or heron as anthropomorphs of the Unknowable, the pre-Christian.

The unfathomable character of the primeval is perceived by the cause-and-effect Christian mind/will as Evil because it is beyond the bounds of our ideas of finite pattern, of action and inevitable consequence, of Justice which is fundamental to the Judeo-Christian mind. Evil is that which we may neither predict nor placate nor prevent; if we confront it we die a tragic heroic death, if we give in to it we die as pawns of the gods, if we ignore it we die as fools. Such is the "pagan" classical view of fate. Me? I don't know what to think. I mean about Evil. Or even Meaning. Now I *try* to look without proving anything. I know I'm a hopeless Romantic who projects human capacities for love and understand onto all creatures. I'm *trying* to be non-teleological, to demythologize my perception, be scientific, detached.

We will not ask, then: What did I do to deserve this? That is absurdity. It was not a "punishment." Rather, we ask: What is this event telling us? Are we capable enough to discover an answer to such a question? Or, we could ask, What did we do/think/feel to bring about this event? We did all we thought we could to avoid an accident. We did everything according to correct nautical procedure, with lights on the sails, running lights, signaling other boats. We knew that barges have channels that they run in. Because we were sailing, we could not avoid tacking across the channels as we made our way against the wind down river. With all the pleasure boats out at night, we didn't expect to see a working barge at midnight.

We could simply accept the general opinion of the unsympathetic: "You shouldn't have been out there in the first place." The river at night is a potentially dangerous place, but so is New York City at any time of the day or night, so is most of the world a dangerous place. Are we to conclude that we are "asking" for trouble simply by being?

MITSUBISHI BEACH

Ah, yes. This reminds me of one of our earliest adventures, the day Ken suggested we paddle all the way across New York Harbor, show off to the folks at the Statue of Liberty (with a kite trailing behind the kayak), and then paddle over to Staten Island. Well, it was terrifically windy and very rough going, and there were ferries and tugs and every other kind of large commercial ship between us and the island; our shoulders were tearing out of their sockets, our forearms burned with carpal tunnel syndrome, we were taking bucketsful of filthy water right in the face, getting sunburnt, hungry....

So we decided to try for Governor's Island and reached it, exhausted, only to discover that, of course, it is impregnable with high cut-stone sea walls all around; we attempted to put up rigging and sail back and nearly capsized as we tried to avoid being battered against the seawall which we were forbidden, by military looking fellows on shore, to touch.

We set out again and were blown far toward the east, with Staten Island in sight but out of reach. A part of New Jersey presented itself and as the tailwind was encouraging us, we put in at a steep sandy beach littered with chunks of cement, driftwood, plastic, rusty pikes, crushed beer cans -- all the usual disgusting mess you find on any shore near New York City. After a treacherous landing, we gingerly carried the Klepper up the beach to a clear flat stretch of sand and proceeded to lay out lunch on a block of concrete. Above us was a little rise of ground rimmed with ragged grass and a very tall chain-link fence topped by razor-wire. As we broke out the chicken and salad and bottled water and fruit, we heard a Voice, amplified, yet fuzzy, like the announcements that come on in the subway: "You can't *be* there!"

Ken and I looked at one another; clearly we *were* there. I stood up and walked toward the top of the dune and looked through the wire. And there was a veritable sea of shiny new cars, Mitsubishi, every single one. And at the far end of this sea of shining metal was a low concrete building with a sign that read: **MITSUBISHI**.

In front of it stood a man in a uniform and a gun and a walkie-talkie and he was walking toward me repeating, "You *can't be* there!" Clearly, he thought we were industrial spies who had suddenly materialized for from his point of view there was no boat to be seen, hidden as it was by the top of the sand dune and the scraggly grass. I shouted back, "But we *are* here! We're just resting, we're having some chicken." I don't think he understood.

We had to eat and pack up in a hurry, carry the Klepper around the bend out of the worst of the wind, find a spot which was relatively free from sharp objects that would pierce the hull or the bottoms of our rubber boots and give us lock-jaw, and so we made a treacherous embarkation and paddled like mad towards the backside of the Statue of

Liberty. I hope he understood that what he was saying was an ontological impossibility, and that when he saw our boat felt a twinge of yearning to *be* one of us.

You see, you never know where you might end up when you get on the water. Change is built in to the paddler's life, as it is for the sailor. That's why it is so important to be organized and ship-shape, for chaos will always win out over order. But all we ask is a reprieve, a time to be, safely, a part of it all, a chance to eat lunch, and to get home again without accident.

The definition of an accident is just that, an accidental occurrence that defies good intentions, good planning, prosper precautions. We put ourselves in jeopardy every time we climb a ladder to change a light bulb, or boil water for tea, or walk the dog, or get into a car or airplane or boat, or ride a bicycle or put on rollerblades. Life is potentially accidental. We do not have absolute control; we can only try our best given our skills within the circumstances. So, Why did we survive *so well*? That is the question.

Sitting safely at the corner desk in my apartment from which I view the Hudson River over the top of my computer screen, my eye strays each time an ocean liner, or barge, or tug, or schooner passes. I always admired the quiet dignity of a boat moving across the static skyline, the sturdy determined character of a tug, the grace of a sailboat, the brute power of a barge churning the grey river to a white froth, the QEII or some other immense white ocean liner majestically sailing up in the pink morning light or down in the orange afternoon and blotting out the entire New Jersey shoreline, bigger than life. Now, I feel a secret awe and even a calm satisfaction that I *know* what it is to move, dolphin-like, beneath the dark poisonous water, beneath the terrible roaring indifference of the force of those man-made Leviathans.

I have been there, conscious and eyes wide open in the Unconscious realms of the phenomenal world, and have learned that we must approach the indifference of the Universe and ask it to speak through us. Perhaps through art we can become translucent.

Once, back in the mid-60s, I tried LSD. We need so many years to see the patterns of the waves of our secret inner selves. I have heard that Leonardo da Vinci had special powers of concentration so that he could slow down his visual, could see the details of the wing motions of a bird in flight, could slow down and draw the patterns of swirling water, of relentless waves, had immediate *understanding by observation* of the physical world, so that he could record them, study them, draw conclusions in order to utilize what he learned. He was able to look without trying first to prove anything; he proved plenty later, after having looked, really looked.

The signatures of our mental world, conversely, we translate into physical signs or there is a "manifestation" from the universe; sometimes we are slow to understand there is a pattern forming. It was my first trip to Long Island; I was still living in land-locked Columbus, Ohio, where the Olentangy River was no consolation for the loss of the Lake Erie vacations of my childhood. My Poet friend, whom I had met at Woodstock two years before, drove us out one hot shimmering day for a weekend on the shore. (He was then working at the Eighth Street Bookstore where the Old Cedar Bar used to be in the days when Eighth Street was civilized.) We drove the ninety miles to Montauk from his Brooklyn flat and got a motel room on the beach for Saturday night. We explored the fish markets on Saturday and planned to spend all Sunday on the beach. This was in May of 1968 and the beaches were still empty of summer people, the water was still almost too cold for swimming.

My Poet friend was in a group in New York City that used LSD as part of the therapy; they read what Timothy Leary their guide suggested, mainly *The Tibetan Book of the Dead* by Evans-Wentz, and listened to "Lucy in the Sky with Diamonds" by the Beatles as a psychedelic song. Although I had been surrounded by The Drug Culture since leaving high school in 1961--indeed many of my college friends at Ohio State were users or even dealers in grass, heroin, uppers, downers, all colors of pills. In the days of the Beats, reading Kerouac in high school, hearing about Haight-Ashbury from Cousin Bill, I was nevertheless almost totally innocent about drugs and their effects. I hated being drunk and indulged only in a few puffs of passing joints at parties, "to be sociable."

That I was a young mother had something to do with my reticence, my sense of responsibility to keep my head and my health. But that was only part of the picture, for I wanted badly to become a professor and a Writer. My curiosity generally took the form of Observer rather than Researcher when it came to drugs. And I was skeptical, rather like Lewis Carroll's humorless and sober-minded Alice surrounded by the fantastic creatures beyond the Looking Glass. By nature, I am slow to change and stubbornly resist fashion. The Pill, panty-hose (which made the mini-skirt viable), false eye-lashes, dawning awareness of the ethical issues of the undeclared war in Viet Nam, Beat Poets in coffee houses, the beginnings of a new terminology: Hippie, Groovy, Peaceniks, Flower Power...all coincided in my awakening consciousness with the discovery of Sartrean existentialism ("Man is free"), Chaucerian humor and humanitarianism (contrasting his Pandarus, of *Troilus and Cresseida* to moralistic Shakespeare!). I was too young to have been a real Beatnik, too stuffy to be a very good Hippie. Yet this was My Generation. I was in it and wanted to be *of* it, too; that commune in Woodstock in 1966 had been a gesture. *Faux geste.*

Once we had our blanket spread on the sand at Montauk beach and were settled in for a Sunday on the seashore, my Poet friend took from his plaid shirt pocket a tiny packet in which were wrapped two pieces of tissue soaked with dots of LSD. On an impulse, I said, "Don't leave me behind, let me take half a dose. I want to know what this is like." I recalled that my kindly psychologist had told me that, if I ever did try taking drugs, she believed that I would be all right. Her trust in me gave courage.

A full dose of LSD is supposed to last twelve hours, my Poet friend told me. So, I figured that my half-dose would last six hours. Therefore, I reasoned, I would become "sober" before he did and thus be able to drive us back to Brooklyn at the end of the day. So I thought.

He tore one of the tiny LSD-soaked pieces of tissue paper in half and I let it dissolve on my tongue like a communion wafer. I lay back on the blanket to enjoy the morning sun and began to think about food. We had some tinned meat, a tiny loaf of cocktail pumpernickel, sardines, that sort of thing. I decided to walk over the dunes to the IGA and get some fresh fruit and salad.

Inside the immense empty supermarket, I felt disoriented but found my way with the support of a large shopping cart to the produce at the back of the store; mounds of pulsating cantaloupe and honeydew melons beckoned.

It was beginning to dawn on me that the drug was already taking effect. This was not like being tipsy. I wanted to be back on the blanket in the open air and talk with my Poet friend about what would happen. Everything green was merging and waving; I couldn't' distinguish lettuce from spinach from leeks. I picked out one of the friendlier melons, took a melon-ball maker (a two-ended chrome spoon that looked like a miniature ice-cream scoop) from a rack above, picked up a box of cherry tomatoes, and made for the check-out counter which by now was several miles away near the door. I suddenly had to pee. With my squirming sack of fruit clutched under one arm, I managed to negotiate my way across an immense four-lane highway to the Gulf station opposite. In the ladies' room I took care of Nature's call and then leaned over the sink to splash my face with water and started to plait my windblown hair into a single braid. When my eyes met my eyes-in-the-mirror they were caught up in a Bridget Riley-esque pattern of undulating black and white squares; the bathroom was tiled entirely in one-inch black and white ceramic tiles which were beginning to absorb me into their order.

With a tremendous effort of will, I gathered up my spherical friends who were yearning to be freed from their bag, wrenched open the door and staggered through the intense morning sunshine, again crossed the by-now busy four-lane highway, traversed the endless bright parking lot, climbed the mountain range of dunes, and rode my trusty camel across yellow undulating sands toward the oasis of our blanket where my Poet friend lay blissfully unaware of my heroic mission.

I held that cantaloupe in my hands and marvelled at its pulsating pattern of squiggly flesh. I lay stretched on my back while it rested on my stomach and I closed my eyes. I made a tent by holding my light cotton shirt high above my head with outspread fingers and the light pierced it gently with golden darts. I became a pier, my bones became the sturdy weather-worn pilings of a pier that jutted far out into the sea; the flesh on my bones melted away to reveal the pure structure the pier of myself to which boats attached themselves, under which fish swam and seabirds nested. I opened my eyes and the clouds were full of faces, the faces of babies, the angelic faces of smiling *putti* of all hues--brown, pink, yellow, red, and black. I thought of the collage on the sleeve of the Beatles' *Sergeant Pepper* album. Eventually, I stripped down to my black wool knit bathing suit and waded into the water.

The beach was empty except for a fisherman down there wearing high rubber waders and casting his line far out into the gentle surf. I swam until the water was just above my shoulders when I touched bottom with my toes. I turned to see my dozing Poet friend, our blanket home, tufts of grey-green hair growing along the bald rim of the undulating dunes. I thought of our barber in my small home town in Ohio. In his window was a white china head of a man with green grass growing out of tiny holes all over his shiny white scalp.

I turned again and looked out to sea, my head level with an infinite horizon. If I kept swimming straight ahead I might reach Ireland (where I had yet to go); if I kept swimming I would become a dolphin. I *knew* this. I could concentrate on The Great White Light of Undifferentiated Consciousness that I had just read about in *The Tibetan Book of the Dead*, translated by Evans-Wentz with an introduction by Jung back at my poet friend's Brooklyn apartment, and then I would not become anything. But I wanted to be *in* the world, to be a corporeal thing, to live, to feel, to swim, to be free--anything at all, but to *be*.

I decided I *would* become a dolphin after all; my body became one powerful integrated muscle, I took in a gulp of air, exhaled noisily through the opening between my eyes, made an arching dive and headed out into the deep water. But then, what about my little boy who was up in Canada vacationing with his grandparents? What about my studies? What about my Poet friend who would eventually wake up and find that I was not there to drive us back? What about my pet cantaloupe keeping cool and murmuring to itself under my white shirt?

I swam parallel to the beach, back and forth, and kept my eyes fixed on the ridge of dunes that would keep me anchored in this life, this particular life which was only one of many embedded and simultaneously expanding existences on the sphere of space-time, as my old friend Alex, a philosophy student at the time, had purportedly discovered back in Columbus during one of *his* "trips."

There was more that happened that day, mostly in the respective minds of myself and my Poet friend, incoherent data which evaporated into psychedelic limbo after twelve hours. I tried to "rescue" my Poet friend from sunstroke late in the afternoon.

He is six foot five. And he was beginning to panic. I discovered that when I attempted to exercise my will in contradiction to the "givens" the images that spontaneously and relentlessly appeared without my controls. I could not speak, and the surrounding benevolent scenery turned violently threatening.

When I got my Poet friend's arm over my shoulder and our selves over the dunes, slipping and sliding and me half dragging him, and then into the passenger seat of his station wagon, and had put myself in the driver's seat, I attempted to reach the gas pedal (his legs were very long and the seat was pushed back too far for me), I pulled the choke and started to turn the ignition key. The wildflowers and grass on the dunes surrounded the car and attacked, the other cars in the IGA parking lot became sharks with gleaming steel teeth instead of radiator grilles. I could not explain, I could only realign myself with the surge of relentless images that once again became lovely, funny, full of wonder. In order to comfort my overheated Poet friend, I fed him the cherry tomatoes one by one and let him hold my flowered cotton hanky. I watched with fascination as he rapidly aged into an old man, a skeleton and then became an infant, a child, and himself once again.

Half a dose of LSD lasted just as long as a full dose, as it turned out, and it was much more than twelve hours which included a mad midnight drive back to Brooklyn in fast bumper-to-bumper traffic which included careening limos and a fatal motorcycle accident on the L.I.E. (my Poet friend drove after all) before we would crowd naked together over his kitchen washbasin like two wild deer, creatures at a desert watering place, to frantically scrub the sand and hallucinations from our skin. I was glad of the experience, yet was never again interested in taking drugs. Even in the midst of the apparent mental realities, I knew that, in relation to the world of matter (which includes my body) they were illusion; my physical self and that of my Poet friend could not, *should* not, travel where the "tripping" mind went, not without irreversible consequences.

The mind must be a good parent and protect the child-body, the innocent dependent struggling flesh, our creaturehood.

Thus, I have severe doubts about the virtual reality of computerized experiences we now have--forty-odd years later. Part of a plot, perhaps, to prepare the human race to turn its back on nature and responsibility, to prepare us for life in outer space when all we need be is a head with two hands attached.

"THE FASCINATION OF WHAT'S DIFFICULT"

The challenge to the artist -- to manifest visions and ideals in the communicable materials of the world, in paint, stone, language--is the challenge to every human being. To turn imagination into a workable reality, to make our dreams manifest. To reverse the process and expect the frailty of matter to follow the virtual realities of phantasy is to court disaster. I believed this then, and now, with "virtual reality" become a computer-reality, I believe it still; we must never lose our authentic communion with Nature.

ALISON ARMSTRONG

In that youthful foolhardiness I did learn, just as the youthful Arthur learned from his mentor Merlin, in T.H. White's delightful "biography" *The Once and Future King*, what it is to be another Being. Arthur was turned into creatures that inhabit all the elements in order to expand his education, for a broader sympathy with all beings within his future kingdom. I know what it is to be a dolphin, not, alas, because I had Merlin as tutor, but because of the time I spent in the ocean under the influence of a psychedelic fungus, ergot. Who is to disprove me, when I demonstrated this "knowledge" to save my life in the Hudson River more than twenty years later? It seems that the mind stores and provides the body with information, however strangely gained: what a dolphin feels and does within its own body form (so perfectly adapted to life in the sea). Or what Lloyd Bridges must have felt like, when, in the TV program I watched in 1955 after school after the Mouseketeers and he dived to avoid the propellers of the bad guy's boat.

And the body, like a dutiful and curious child, uses the information anew, to act in the world for its own benefit. It's a matter, not of Mind *over* Matter, but of Mind *nurturing* Matter. If we mentally decided to physically go uptown to buy a material toy that has spiritual significance to our hypothetical Inner Child, why should the process stop there, to be dismissed as mere "symbolic gesture?"

The metaphor is the foundation stone of human learning, I believe. Symbols have latent significance, gestures have unforeseen consequences, and the spiritual, the mental realities, manifest themselves in the "real" world of events, relationships, and material things. A poem, the idea of a garden of stones and water, a sculpture, a toy, a boat...all these took me to Maine. And back.

Vico's Age of Gods still lives, the time when, as the ancients knew, *all things are full of gods.* This is not to deny the subsequent Age of Heroes (action) and Age of Man (thought). They too, as we know, are very much the motive forces of our western civilization. But the earliest forms of consciousness -- awe, *super*stition (not *sus*picion), belief in the parallel worlds of the spiritual and the material -- expressed by way of metaphor, of resemblances taken literally, and gave us the truths of mythology. There is a "latent content" as well as a "manifest content" to our existence. If we resist this Freudian language and reject Freud's insights, we throw out the baby with the bath water, for Freud understood what Bergson, and before him Giambattista Vico, articulated: there is more than one way to acquire understanding. Freud claimed (in, for example, *The Future of an Illusion*) that he was not "religious" and that he never *experienced* what he observed in others, the *Oceanic feeling*. His loss.

The knowledge I gained from daring to "let go," in surrendering to the Oceanic, even if only occasionally, in accepting the realities of my dream images, my hallucinogenic experience, my Inner Child's desire, stood me in good stead as much as any book learning ever did. A quarter of a century after my "becoming" an LSD dolphin off the beach at Montauk, I would find it both necessary and possible to dive into the vortex beneath that barge.

And when I feel the urge to set out alone in my own ***Skidbladther,*** up the Hudson fjord above Bear Mountain Bridge beyond World's End and beneath the solid presence of Storm King Mountain--as across the clear cold green water of Bass Harbor toward the playground of the seals--I know that nothing is lost on us, that everything we experience has some "sense." We find a way to give a form perceptible to others. Something to write about is taking its course.

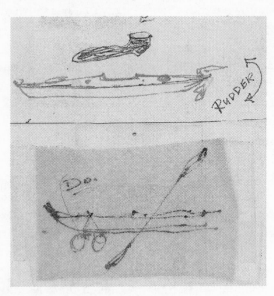

--Alison Armstrong
Maine, New York City & Beacon, NY
1992

THE PHANTOM BARGE

On July 3rd, 1990, Ken and I set sail on the Hudson River in his seventeen-foot folding kayak. We had put in around 4:30 p.m. (just before high tide) at Pier 36 planning to sail the kayak up river with the flood tide and paddle back down with the ebb around 10:30 p.m. We had rigged the kayak with new leeboards, running lights, aluminum mast and boom, mainsail and jib. We packed dry-bags with first-aid kit, a pocket flashlight, waterproof lantern, flares, whistle, dry clothing, food, and drinking water. Each of us wore a Type II Personal Floatation Device.

Sailing up river with a stiff southwesterly wind was beautiful. By 7:30 we reached a tiny beach on the New Jersey shore north of George Washington Bridge, stopped for a picnic supper, then continued north beyond the Cloisters. The Palisades glowed orange-red in the twilight of a perfect summer evening; a nearly full moon rose over Manhattan. Colorful sparks from fireworks too far away to hear illuminated the horizon. Pleasure boats greeted us; an occasional barge passed regally pushed by a sturdy tug.

As twilight turned to darkness, I signaled other boats with our nine-volt marine lantern shining it on the sails. Red-and-green running lights were on the cross-section of the leeboards, and Ken had a small light fixed on the stern.

The moon rose high over the GW Bridge. At 10:00, we decided to turn with the tide and sail back down river as long as we could, tacking against the wind. The beamy wood and canvas kayak felt very stable under sail. We were making such good time that we were reluctant to switch to paddling. Since the tide had not completely turned and the wind was still coming from the southwest, we estimated that we'd pass beneath the bridge sailing southward after four tacks. But in fact we made our way under the massive bridge on the second tack and got a close view of the little red lighthouse under the supporting steel pillars on the New York shore. Although we had the right-of-way over motorized vessels, we were prepared to give way to larger, faster boats. A motorized converted paddle-wheeler, blaring dance music, looped around us several times; the lively passengers waved and called out to us each time they passed. We responded, waving our lights, as we continued to tack against the wind in a broad herringbone pattern over oncoming waves. We were making good progress under sail as we approached 125th Street when the wind increased and the water became turbulent, battering our hull with noisy chop. We made good speed when heading directly into the waves on the southwesterly tack but shipped water over the starboard when tacking toward the southeasterly New York shore. My PFD made it difficult to maneuver, so I removed it and placed it between my knees.

At about midnight, after nearly an hour of intense sailing through heavy water, the waves seemed to subside a bit; as we came about on the New Jersey side Ken decided it would be better to finish the next southeasterly tack at the 79th Street Boat Basin where we could rest and stow the mast and sails. We could then paddle down river close to the Manhattan short to Pier 26. On the last tack in mid-river, as we prepared to scan the water again for other boats, Ken, at the rudder, looked over his left shoulder, then cried out, "Quick, give me my paddle!"

I swung around from my seat in the bow where I was controlling the jib; with my left hand I reached to untoggle Ken's paddle and at the same time lifted my lamp with my right arm. A dark wall of steel, some 30 feet high, was bearing down on us. It seemed to come from nowhere. It had no lights and no one was on it to call out to. We had only an instant to act. I called out to Ken, "No time!" It was too late to change course. No time for complete sentences, let alone tactical debate. Expecting to feel the crunch of a thousand tons of steel on my backbone, I rose from my seat and dove over the right leeboard, intending to swim to New Jersey.

I don't recall hitting the water, but I remember taking the first stroke in an effort to get away while glancing over my right arm and seeing the steel wall. Then foaming water flooded over my eyes and a sucking power pulled me backward and under. Despite attempts to swim, I was sucked into a churning vortex beneath the massive dark hull. The incessant dull roar of motors surged above me. I felt the barge's steel hull rub against my back. My fleece jacket seemed to snag on something rough.

I envisioned a propeller coming up soon, knew I must dive or get chopped to bits by blades perhaps as big as myself. I opened my eyes and, working against instinct, exhaled and dove as deeply as I could with empty lungs. The filthy water around me had a greenish glow. I could see dancing bubbles of my breath leaving for the surface. I rejected an impulse to breathe in, amazed I was able to keep from gasping for air for so long.

"Just this moment, keep alive *this* moment," I told myself.

Finally the pressure that held me beneath the hull let up. I bobbed to the surface into the black silky night air. As soon as I surfaced, I heard Ken's choking voice calling my name. I turned toward the departing roar and saw Ken's head bobbing among the waves as the blunt back end of a huge barge, pushed on the opposite rear corner by a white tugboat, plowed on down river, its crew –if it had any—unaware of us tiny creatures struggling in its wake. I floated on my back to rest and saw random stars overswept by gathering clouds.

Everything became very still except for the surging waves and occasional dull thud of bursts of distant fireworks over Manhattan. As we swam toward one another in the dark, I saw that Ken could barely keep his head above water. I ripped open the zipper of my water-logged fleece jacket and tore if off my arms impatiently, thinking that I must get hold of Ken, support his head in a fireman's rescue grip perhaps, if he'd let me, and try to swim somewhere before we both went under. I shouted, "Where's our boat?"

Ken spotted the black rubber hull of the overturned kayak floating about ten yards from us down river. His windbreaker was tight at the wrists and holding in water so that he could not lift his arms to swim. By dog- paddling, he reached the kayak and kept calling for me. I swam through the darkness until I reached his side. Together we managed to rock the kayak once, and it righted itself immediately. The mast and sails were underwater, dragging at the kayak that was half full of water but afloat. I hooked my left arm over the starboard coaming and attempted to kick myself free of the rigging, which tangled around my legs. Ken got astride the stern and handed me the small flashlight that was still in a pocket of his windbreaker.

I shone it hoping to attract the attention of other boats. But by now, just past midnight, there was no river traffic—except another dark barge pushing up river along the Manhattan shore. We cried out, "Help!" over and over, but that barge continued on, like a robot or ghost. The possibility of being struck and run over a second time overwhelmed us with horror.

We were exactly in mid-river. Ken took his paddle and attempted to direct the kayak toward the Manhattan side. We soon realized that we would not be able to paddle to shore before the combined forces of the relentless river current and out-going tide had swept us past Westbeth, past Pier 26, past all of Manhattan.

Ken opened the repair kit hanging from the gunwale and took out the flares. While waves, blown up river, inundated the kayak and splashed into our faces, he attempted to read by feeble moonlight the tiny printed instructions. The first flare went off quickly and burned his finger. He fired the remaining two flares held aloft, but they were no competition for the sporadic early Independence Day fireworks now exploding over the city. With nothing left to use but a whistle and the tiny flashlight, we decided that he should signal S.O.S. on the whistle and I would keep shining the flashlight. We watched our large marine lantern float down-river bobbing out of reach, beaming its strong light uselessly at the sky. The waves that kept washing over us from the south did nothing to slow the pull of outgoing tide that moved us relentlessly toward New York Harbor. We were being washed out to sea.

Ken had been struck in the back of the head so it was difficult for him to keep his balance astride the stern of the kayak while he paddled and blew S.O.S. on his marine whistle. I retrieved my life jacket, the waterproof food bag, and a dry bag that floated around in the swamped kayak and stuffed them into the prow to give it some buoyancy while I continued to cling with my left elbow to the wooden gunwale. My fingers were going numb. We'd been over-run by the barge at about 80th Street, and were now being carried past 34th Street. Waves were washing away our body heat, our strength, and ability to think.

Eventually, we saw a cluster of lights and heard voices. A glowing white cabin cruiser, brilliantly lit, drew near, its engine idling. At first I was uncertain whether it saw us or was going to run over us, but soon we realized that it was slowly and steadily circling in. Four young men leaned over the side. Their presence seemed as sudden and benevolent as the barge's appearance had been sudden and brutal. I managed to swim along to the prow of our kayak and retrieve its towline while the boys pulled Ken aboard. They reached for me with a pole, then pulled me up gleaming chrome steps into their bright white Criscraft. I handed them the line and collapsed. I saw that Ken, wrapped in a large towel, was bleeding from a gash on the back of his head.

We sat shivering while our rescuers alerted the Coast Guard on their radio. The Coast Guard responded, saying that their presence was not necessary since no one was killed and "only a kayak" was involved. (Their policy, we were told, is not to investigate damage to boats worth less than $25,000.) Our four rescuers good-naturedly begged us not to put their names in any newspaper. They had borrowed the cabin cruiser, which belonged to one of their fathers, without permission. One of the anonymous young men said, "I had this premonition it would be just our luck to have to rescue somebody tonight when we are not supposed to be out like this." But what good luck that they were!

After a muffled radio conversation with the Coast Guard, the young men revved the motor and headed for New Jersey with the kayak in tow. We watched helplessly as most of our possessions washed away. They wrapped us in dry towels and took us inside the warm cabin.

Then we went ashore at the Imperial Marina in Weehawken where we stepped into a freezing air-conditioned ambulance. The young paramedics seemed to be interested only in repeatedly taking our blood pressure despite the blare of rock music from the ambulance radio.

We fared no better in the emergency room—nobody seemed to understand that we were possibly in shock, cold and soaked with filthy river water, that Ken was still bleeding from his head wound. No one thought to get us dry or clean or warm. The first order of protocol was to put us into wheelchairs and interview us at length about our insurance status while we sat unattended in the air-conditioned deserted lobby.

I finally insisted that Ken be treated for his wound. When I tried to follow him through the flapping green doors to a silent vast ER, hospital staff held me back, but eventually also let me in and gave me a gown and a bed in a cubicle next to Ken's. A nurse joked, "How'd you hold your breath so long? Sure is a good thing you don't smoke. Anything I can get you?" I longed for a cigarette and a cup of hot coffee with cream, but had to be content with an aspirin and a paper cup of weak tea. I also longed for a hot shower and a tampon, but was given just a thin cotton sheet to cover up with. After what seemed hours of intense listening for sounds of life from Ken who lay behind a curtain getting stitches, a sympathetic male nurse reunited us.

At 4:30 a.m. on the morning of the 4th of July, we were released from St. Mary's ER. The nurse told us we could now phone a neighbor to come and pick us up. Clearly she lived in suburbia, not in New York City. We woke up the only friend in Lower Manhattan we knew who had a vehicle, but he was too sleepy to understand what Ken was explaining on the phone. So, barefoot, wearing nothing but faded cotton hospital gowns (that tie at the back and flap open), without money, carrying our few sodden belongings in clear plastic bags, we walked out of the hospital and into a taxicab. On the way to Manhattan, inside the Holland Tunnel where he could not turn around, we announced to the driver that we had money at home but none with us. He waited at the curb while Ken and I took turns running up to our respective apartments to find what cash we could to pay him. After hot showers and clean clothes, we celebrated our escape with a large omelette and pot of coffee in Ken's kitchen.

Next day, we drove to New Jersey in Ken's old station wagon and retrieved his kayak and his water-soaked wallet from the Imperial Marina, Weehawken. No white cabin cruiser was in sight. We dried out the contents of his wallet on the dashboard in the sun, dismantled the kayak, and returned home. And began to ask questions. A Coast Guard lieutenant told Ken that there are unlit barges engaged in illegal traffic at night on the Hudson. The police department in the precinct that includes West 80th Street (near where we were struck) recorded the "incident" as "a case of hit and run." To us, the barge remains a phantom—a reminder of the prudence required of boaters on a large body of water where commercial traffic not only adds to the complexities of currents, winds, and tides, but also takes precedence over pleasure boating. We continued for a while to paddle and sail on the Hudson, but never after dark. Later that summer, we got out of town and went to Maine by way of the pristine lakes of the Adirondacks.

--Alison Armstrong,
Originally published in *Sea Kayaker* magazine (Summer 1991) *[Revised July & Sept. 2010]*

A WAY OF MAKING TEA:
Excerpts from a Country Diary

*"Even when you are in circumstances of need, do not feel that
your situation is inconvenient or dissatisfying. Being in a difficult
situation and yet not to think of it as being so, this is Wabi."*
--Sotan, Grandson of Sen Rikyu [1]

THE RAIN DROPPED lazily onto the lilac leaves outside my window. I knew the magnificence, variety, and ultimate simplicity of the universe. And then I opened my eyes.

I awaken, here in the Endless Mountains. Chaotic thoughts intrude on my silence, and I turn toward the window. A gentle warm rain is falling. I can hear the large drops hit the leaves of the lilac bush. A line of poetry flies to comfort me: "It is the banana leaf that speaks of it first...." Yes, and "the sound of the rain needs no translation." The random drops, do they have a pattern that is beyond comprehension? Does Chaos Theory apply? Gentle randomness feels so lovely. Not being able to anticipate the next sound keeps me in the moment. I settle back into the morning's beauty. To see what the day brings. Present expectations, what to do in the garden, in the studio) mingle with memories of adventures that occurred without much planning: the LSD trip at Montauk in May 1966; the barge confrontation 3rd July 1990; the death of husband Robert the next day; the death nine years later of my companion another Robert; the loss of our house, our garden, our dreams.... But our time together was fortuitous.

Is it true that we make our own reality, not only over the course of a life but also from day to day, moment to moment. What a responsibility! Like a child being urged never for a moment to doubt that Peter Pan can fly, so it seems with us and our daily realities for which we are responsible. "Nothing true but thinking makes it so," as Hamlet says?

Accomplishments occur spontaneously as well as after rigorous work. Duration of effort does not guarantee success. Often the spontaneously produced results are the most satisfying, the most beautiful, the truest: a Japanese pinch-pot, a perfect enso a zen circle, brushed in sumi ink, a photograph when we clicked a camera at just the right moment. Even an accident can bring happy results.

In Old Japan, my favorite shop on Bleecker Street in New York, I discovered Alex Kerr's memoir, *Lost Japan,* and was enchanted by the following experience he had during tea ceremony with Sawada Minoru, tea master at Oomoto:

> The tea used in the ceremony is finely powdered green tea, carried in a lacquered caddy called a Natsume which is shaped like an egg with a flat bottom and top. One day, a student failed to support the body of the caddy, taking only the lid in his hands, and the caddy dropped from the height of about one meter directly onto the tatami. The powdered tea puffed up high into the air in a cloud, and tea settled in a green ring on the mat before our startled eyes.... In silence, Sawada asked us, 'What is the appropriate thing to say at a time like this'? Nobody could answer. He said, 'You should say, 'How beautiful'! And indeed, the ring of powdered green tea on the mat *was* beautiful. Sawada told us to gather around and look at it. 'You may never see this again in all your lives', he said. '.... Look and admire' ! Then, after we had looked, Sawada kept us on for a lesson in how to clean the tatami....[3]

We sometimes notice the imaginative powers in small accidental ways: we decide to mail an envelope with a bill in it. As we are lifting it to the letterbox, we have second thoughts: perhaps we should wait a few days to make sure there will be enough money in our checking account. The envelope falls to the ground like a forgotten leaf. Did we mean to mail it or not mail it? Our indecision confused it. Ambivalent thoughts yield ambivalent results. A lack of mindfulness does not prevent consequences.

Another example: when you are riding a horse, it is well known that you cast your eyes where you intend to go and the horse responds. If you are exercising in the ring and want him to trot into the corner you do not look at the center, you look at that corner. You do not look at the ground where you do not want to be. If you want to canter into the center to change leads and direction, you cast your eyes into the center of the ring while you are still riding at the wall. The horse will follow your eyes. Your eyes are your intentions. Your energy follows your eyes.

MC Richards (poet, potter, educator, and author of several books including *Centering: In Poetry, Pottery, and the Person*) wrote that one's life is the "the Big Art." She gained her wisdom from her own life which was filled with changes, recoveries, involvement in the early days of Black Mountain College, later guest teaching at Haystack and universities in America and England, discovering the Rudolf Steiner Waldorf schools, writing poetry, working clay on the potter's wheel as a literal mode of centering and as metaphor. I glance at her books[4] on the shelf by the bed. I am living in what was once her house. I try to meditate without moving in my cosy bed, lulled by the repetitious sounds of rain.

I awake again, with the title of this essay in my head and an image of a pale yellow label pasted onto a little private press book. Like a sleepwalker, I move into the study, sit at my desk, and begin spontaneously to write I know not what. I am still in that liminal place between dream and waking. I resist my old impulse from years of scholarly duties, of gathering books. For confidence. For references. For inspiration, and to waste time, postpone, perhaps lose my way. If I pile up books written by others too soon, I may never come to the validity and possible pain of my own thoughts. That old attempt at ordering my efforts through research, derived from too many years in graduate school, would create a chaotic anxiety, turn this freedom into a burden.

Likewise in my art studio, I am most inhibited when I surround myself with images by others. But I have them, not from a wish to imitate, but from a desire to be reminded of my own visions that come in the dark, or to capture an essence or a particular technique, say, of Leonardo's *sfumato,* or the deep space implicit in the nuances of ancient Japanese landscapes -- ink on silk or rubbed gold or tarnished silver leaf. I attempt these effects in various mediums without benefit of the 400 or 600 years of aging that contributed to the results I so admire. Aesthetic emotion thrills me.

Likewise, in potting. Japanese potters and folk art collectors Roshanjin, Hamada, and Soetsu Yanagi were enchanted by ancient folk pottery, "imperfect" Korean and Japanese tea bowls. They and we look closely, not to imitate, but rather to absorb their essence, to allow their uniqueness to permeate our awareness, the wisdom of ancient craftsmen, their love of the material, their respect for spontaneous manipulation of clay into simple elegance. "Ordinary mind" energy of hand-and-eye worked with the fire to achieve what the clay wants.

I am humbled in the presence of a simplicity so difficult to achieve. I approach my studio as if entering a teahouse, dampen the grey moss growing on the big stones by the door. I cautiously greet the snake that lives beneath the stepping stone. My mood is meditative. I lay out my materials and hold in mind the images from dreams or meditation that have come to me for the work in progress, or to experiment. Frequently I begin something new morning but later am faced with a number of issues to solve as the amount of work increases. These images will change as I work; the materials will change them. These images want to be manifested all at once; they are forgetting I am often slowed by thought and by the vicissitudes of time, a physical body that must move through space, and materials that require skill.

It is very difficult to copy the images in the mind. They are a point for beginning. One begins and continues.

I seek out the simplicity of sumi ink, brushes, exquisite paper. My respect for the beauty of the materials stops the mind. Grind the ink, prepare the spirit, steady the hand. Silence. Then action. I walk away while the work completes itself. I return to discover what the ink wanted.

In a recent *Yoga International* magazine I read in Patanjali's yoga sutra what I wish I'd learned years ago:

> You must find a support for the mind before you withdraw it from the external world.... If there are no worldly objects with which to identify, then it identifies with its own thought processes.... Soon it will get bored with nothingness, and... the crafty aspect of the mind will come forward to fill the

void with imaginary objects, fooling you into believing that you are having a spiritual experience.

How many of the objects with which I fill my studio are only the result of my "crafty mind" substituting yet another image for a genuine meditation session? I try to keep my rooms free from clutter, for the clutter of my mind is all too eager to fill my spaces, especially the studio, with irrelevant attempts toward achieving my vision.

I water the potted gardenia bush that blesses this space with its fragrant waxy white blossoms. I settle down with a cup of tea and wait; and then I am working silently. I have learned that there are other ways than Patanjali's to meditate—counting breaths, walking meditation—and learn how the immersion of working in oil on canvas is very different from the methods of Japanese sumi ink on washi. Every medium has its demands and its lessons. The collaboration with the materials is an occasion for meditation. It says: "Who are you?"

I yearn to see the world consistently through Zen eyes. *Shibui.*

Now my mind, as in W.B. Yeats' poem, *A Long Legged Fly*, "moves upon silence." But then, the final lines of another Yeats poem, *Lapis Lazuli*, come to mind due to my impulse to paint mountains, as in old scrolls, with a hut tucked into a fold of landscape. Yeats imagines tiny ancient Chinese monks climbing toward a hut on a mountain path implicit in the texture of the stone.

> *Their eyes, mid many wrinkles, their eyes,*
> *Their ancient, glittering eyes, are gay.*

I make more tea to celebrate my solitude, to ground me.

As in meditating, writing, painting, the tea ceremony is a way of perception. But there is a particular aesthetic that evokes a bittersweet nostalgia, clears a physical and mental space and we experience a humble and ephemeral material world. *Wabi.*

Mutable natural materials of wood, clay, charcoal, iron, water, flower, stone, and grass have been crafted into artifacts with an apparent minimum of artifice (hut, pot, tea bowls, fire, *ikebana* offering, garden path, stone lantern, thatch and fence). *Sabi.* The elegant ritual of Tea is a paradox; established tradition creates a socially leveling experience among a chosen few. And between one's self and one's Self. *Wabi-Sabi.*

My friend M has mastered in photography a Leonardo-esque *sfumato*. He says I should paint every day, it is a long road between the private vision and accomplishing it. That is what mystic painter Agnes Martin also knew. To paint, to write, to work in the darkroom, as to make tea, means getting quiet, being aware in the moment, letting go of the screeching noise of chaos to let order happen through us, communicating through our materials...practicing *Wabi*.

In our extroverted western society, the inner eye, the intuitive, the love of nature and of simplicity are generally submerged. Certainly devalued. The ability to sit quietly is being bred out of our young, who, it would seem, are being "trained" by video games, by television, by computers, palm pilots, electronic toys and devices of all sorts to eventually lead rather sterile lives devoid of direct experience of the natural world; they will travel in space ships and inhabit manmade communities orbiting beyond our blue planet. The lives of future generations may be spent in the service of sophisticated machines. And yet here *I* sit, indoors at a computer screen, typing these thoughts on an electronic keyboard while all of glorious nature calls from every bright window, and ink and brushes and clean sheets of paper in the studio are yearning to be brought together.

SUMI-MIND: A MIND LIKE CHARCOAL

In the early moments of a recent morning meditation, when thoughts were rushing, vying for a sticking place before I would perhaps achieve a letting go, it occurred to me that the ideal state, even function, of mind would be to make the mind like fine charcoal.

I had recently printed out information from a web-site in Japan [5] about charcoal and wood vinegar after attending a lecture on the uses of bamboo one evening earlier in the year at The Japan Society. As a consequence I joined the American Bamboo Society thinking to grow some varieties here at the Pennsylvania farm near the spring where I want to build a teahouse. The web-site information described the special Binchotan charcoal, made from a particular variety of hard and scarce oak from SW Japan; other sumi charcoal is made from bamboo, pieces of which I have hidden in my home. Sumi charcoal gives me metaphors to be perhaps translated into sumi ink.

Sumi charcoal is activated carbon made from natural wood fired at very high temperatures in a clay kiln. It has a long history; used since the 8th century as a fuel, especially in making fine iron tools, iron Buddhist statues, and fittings for temples, as well as for cooking and heating, it is now viewed as an environmentally friendly, ecologically enhancing natural material. It improves our living environments—as an air cleaner, a water purifier, a dehumidifier and deodorizer. Its tissue structure is porous, which makes a perfect home for microbes that absorb contaminants. Sumi also contains minerals and alkaline which are released when used in water.

Because of sumi charcoal's ability to increase negative ions in the air, when placed around the home it will give off a relaxing atmosphere. Some people have put tons of it under new homes before they are constructed; it has been placed in the foundations of some temples that were built hundreds of years ago, the wood of which is still in beautiful condition because the sumi has helped regulate humidity and fended off termites. The beauty of its natural form is used in sculptural ways with dry flower arrangements. Its negative ions prevent "house sickness." Sumi also emits infrared radiation, which warms and stimulates the blood when used in bath water. Its minerals, akin to elements found in natural hot springs, leave the skin soft and silky.

What if our minds could purify our environments so well!

Agnes Martin says that the Mind will tell you all you need to know. She says she contacts Mind when making or looking at art. From the Mind, she says, we learn about happiness and beauty, the essentials of being. Mind is all you need in order to see. She leaves it at that, without using religious words, without psychological terms. For her, there is no prior or external source and no need beyond Mind.

It is axiomatic that this is the source of each individual's being, hence the source of art making, of art appreciation, of living artfully. When we accept her premise, which is also a Zen premise, that Mind is the source of one's basic nature, then we owe ourselves the fulfillment of this simple yet difficult assignment: contact Mind. It is one with the ground of being, beyond petty detail, beyond fretful chores, beyond divisive theory of all sorts.

When I begin to sit in meditation or begin to do something purely for the sake of the activity itself—such as painting, cooking, sculpting, riding, kayaking—just as I am about to go into the studio, or put on an apron in the kitchen, or prepare to change into kayaking or riding gear, the busy crafty monkey-mind presents me with a list of *things I ought to do*: sort laundry, iron, shop, write letters, pay bills, get an oil change, grade papers, toss those leftovers in the fridge, vacuum the house, wash the dog…the list of Oughts and Shoulds is infinite. And never accomplished once and for all. It is subversive.

At the moment, I am gardening, or rather lying in the lawn chair in the garden after having planted a few ornamental grasses. It is too hot to do more. I have meditated, lunched on leftovers. My furry dog Saki is resting in the cool shade recently sprayed with the garden hose where I've planting three painted fern and a yellow striped grass. Saki is dreaming of our impending afternoon walk around Burt's Pond and of the rabbit she will flush from under the blackberry brambles.

How to make one's mind still when even the dog is attributed with preoccupations? How to become like the best Japanese charcoal that purifies water and air, that gives off healthful emanations, that is environmentally friendly in every way, having been tempered in a very hot kiln which (like Hell) burns away all impurities yet leaves the lineaments of the original branch of wood? Can grief and other sorts of suffering (as various rings of Dante's Hell) do that for us? Is suffering necessary for simplicity and purity?

Zen practice teaches that desire, or attachment, is the source of all suffering; a sense of loss is a thwarting of desire, indeed it aggravates desire. Achieving purity through suffering sounds like a western religious idea. We need something more—not additional, but greater, happier, more generous—a willingness to forgive all thwarting of our desires by others, by circumstances, by ourselves, to bring our life activities into harmony with the Way—the Tao. Or, for us westerners, to receive Grace, we learn that we must "Will to will God's will," that Spirit of which we partake, to which we belong.

I imagine each of us as a glowing branch of purified sumi charcoal; I imagine each of us as an aperture in the firmament through which the energy of the Cosmos shines; a black charcoal cosmic space is alive with innumerable sparks of fire.

I sleep profoundly here in the country in MC's farm house while others sleep outside the walls; I do not disturb the deer sleeping in the grassy beds under the old trees. It comforts me to know that they are there, in the two-deer impression beneath the wisteria at the end of my studio, in the eight-deer depression of matted grass under the apple tree behind the long stone wall. During my healing sleeps owls are catching mice, bats are catching insects that fly in the night, the large yellow and brown spider, whose home for the past weeks has been on the remaining dry poppy stalk that I dared not cut for her sake, is bundling her prey into neat silken shrouds for her multitude of ravenous babies. The charcoal in the newly potted dwarf hinoki cypress is purifying the soil; the charcoal in the pitcher is aerating water for Saki and me to drink.

My drowsing brain is sorting and feeding all anticipated tasks, great and small, while the body renews itself. In the morning it will carry me through as many tasks as will fit into a day and an evening. I awake with images for paintings, for writing, for teaching. Are they "crafty-mind" images to mislead me, or metaphors that bring insight? Psychologist Carl Jung advised that it is wise to act out the mental images from "strong" dreams; therefore, he built and lived in the tower, which appeared to him repeatedly in his dreams. In order to discover what the image meant, he made it a real object in the world.[6]

Likewise, if I begin to paint or construct from an image, it is an attempt to see it more closely. What does Mind advise? Where will the ink or paint take us? If we can redirect attention away from the perception of constant interruptions (from the world, from the noise of one's thoughts) and into an image of all activity as interconnected, then the work, the play—duties and delights—cease to be discrete categories. Even all those Oughts and Shoulds on the infinite list of chores become part of a flowing process. Alan Watts has noted that those trained in Zen practice do things without delay.[7]

The impressions that come with me from sleep into conscious daily activities are like the silvery traces of snails on the grey irregular stones of the garden path. I do not recommend living in a formless state, although it is so pleasant to drift into the waking hours, to partake of the rhythms of the season, the cycles of the sun. Soon enough the urgent demands of the city world will have to be met.

There is a structure to the day, whether dictated from without (as in having to wake too soon, turn off the alarm, marshal the day's impedimenta, get dressed, and go off to work) or whether "given" from an inner necessity (with an ear and eye attuned only to the inner messages). Kandinsky, once he had renounced representational painting as the duty of art, insisted on working out of inner necessity.[8] What is it T.S. Eliot said in an essay ("Tradition and the Individual Talent" was it?), that writing from one's inner necessity is more rigorous because we must obey "what is given."

The habitual patterns of days can be made more conscious through ritual—the opposite of dulling habit. Setting aside our duty-bound or compulsive rounds of activities to step into the realm of ritual gives an enriched perspective on the world. The strangeness and mystery of ritual is meant to bring comforting focus and heighten awareness—and ritual is always connected with the two essential experiences of birth and death. Alan Watts, in *Zen and the Beat Way*:

> "Going away, dissolving, is the same thing as living…. A loved one must be allowed to dissolve and not be clung to…such dissolution is the heart of beauty and the heart of life… . That beauty is what the mood of a-war-e in haiku and painting…seeks to evoke."[9]

This way of being "aware" in the ordinary everyday sense, as in times of loss and horror and grief is, I think, essential to our contract with all of existence. It keeps us connected emotionally to that ground of being in which notions of dichotomies, divisive and defensive ideas (personal and political), of enemies, are—if not irrelevant, capable of being defused of their power over us. Ritual, whether sitting in meditation, casting the I-Ching, or reverently making tea for one's self and friends, sets one aside from the irrepressible flow of the river of time-and-action, observing and accepting but not being swept along unconsciously or in helpless panic.

I pace like a cat around my worktable. The smoky scent of sumi ink momentarily reminds me of turf smoke on the air in Ireland. The blackness of the ink, the creamy whiteness of the paper—I want to keep the purity of these elements yet bring them together. It takes courage to load the brush. The marks, once made, may not be altered. They will reveal my state of being in this moment.

My joy in living here in this place is tempered by memory.

In the 1980s I taught courses to foreign students, with all nationalities and languages thrown into the same classrooms; they had come to New York University to master English writing skills that would enable them to be successful in business. One of the essays I chose for discussion was Thoreau's "On the Importance of a Man Building His Own House." This essay was met with contempt or non-comprehension by many of the students, in particular those from Korea, China, and Japan. The very countries whose ancient art now inspires me! These young business students in need of learning English language skills for their future businesses had never lived anywhere but in an urban setting; had never walked in the woods, never made or repaired anything with their hands, never sought solitude in nature. They had no interest in making useful analogies between Thoreau's rustic satisfactions and their own technology-driven world and their expectations based in it. They had no access to or patience with the American romanticizing of Nature and Transcendentalism, of 19th century aesthetic experiences of The Sublime. One young businessman mocked: "If I were to make my own computer from scratch, it would be obsolete by the time I finished it." He saw no value in making a simple dwelling from old materials, straightening bent nails, or growing his own food. There was no virtue, in his eyes, in attempting to become self-sufficient because his world was one of disposable goods, urban conveniences, commerce; an apartment and a meal were always available and the least of his concerns.

But Thoreau's (and my) point was not the recycling of old nails, nor the skills in constructing the little house—it was what could be derived from the process. Why indeed make anything by hand? Thoreau was writing from a tacit assumption that this is good. But, as all craftspeople learn, the commercial returns for hand-made items are often inadequate to the cost in materials and time of labor. It is the process that is of value for the maker. And for me, part of my impulse toward working with the hands is a deep emotional need to recreate the feeling of life on my grandparents' extensive family farm in Ohio. They seemed deeply content; they worked with their hands. Yet were also readers and musicians. I was happy to be with them as a child and was given helping tasks by both grandparents.

It is doubtful whether I was able to instill an appreciation in those NYU business majors for the riches of process that Thoreau sought to convey, unless it was to teach them the joys of revising their essays. When engaged in a repetitive process such as spinning, weaving, potting on a wheel, as Gandhi understood, the process becomes a communion with the self and the creation of harmony, as well as resulting in an end product.

But in all our best-willed efforts we may overlook the one thing for which we may never be forgiven as teacher or parent. "There is no way to be a perfect parent," a psychologist once told me when I worried about what I might be doing wrong in my young son's eyes. There is no way to be a perfect teacher, or artist, or anything else for that matter, since we cannot control the affect of our efforts and communion with others.

Intuition, love, compassion…we throw out self-generated filaments into the world's winds, as with Walt Whitman's "Careful Patient Spider," to "catch Somewhere, Oh my Soul." Will urban business people continue to learn from Nature's examples? With the aid of poetry and visual art as interpreters, perhaps, if direct observation is not possible.

Those who garden or raise animals know they cannot avoid Nature's teachings. Those who make art also should know this. The processes of aware interaction guarantee that we will learn. A child trains the parent as to what is essential. The ritual of a repeated bedtime story is so much more. We need compassionate intuition and an altruistic mind to read the messages of children, or Nature.

There is an Inner Eye that sees what our everyday eye does not; there is an inner comprehension that, as Samuel Beckett put it, "Something is taking Its course." The best relationships, the best meals, the best art, the best results in any activity are the results of a wisely "planned accident." Being centered, acting intuitively and spontaneously in the moment brings surprising manifestations. When free from doubt, anxiety, and fear…those great inhibitors, those creators of pain, strife, attachment, and confusion… our visions can manifest. We are creatures at times brutally shunted from one way of living into another. Desire thwarted is very painful.

I recently met a wise artist whose life had, like mine, "fallen apart" due to the sudden death of his companion. He was losing his home, his studio, his community. And yet he was very calm. Over a wonderful dinner he prepared, he commented that most Americans think they must Do in order to Be. But, he said, it is the other way around. "You must Be in order to Do." True for art making, and true for every other enterprise. I decided that he was probably an angel, that brave man whose surname is Best. He disappeared into his new life after telling me something of value. We attract specific people and events not only from time to time, but continuously as our lives vibrate.

In the summer of 1989, when I should have been finishing my dissertation, I experienced an excruciating depression and vowed to

ALISON ARMSTRONG

give up reading and writing for three months. Instead I began to construct sculptures that derived from a series of strong dreams and mental images of landscapes inspired by a long interest in Japan and by my experiences of Ireland (where I went for academic research, to give papers at conferences, or take courses in Dublin).

In the middle of that non-verbal summer, I was instructed by a psychic to keep all negative feelings and images out of my artwork, for—she said—whatever I put into my art would manifest itself in my life. Within five months of beginning this new activity, I had sold my first large sculpture, met significant new artist friends—and completed the dissertation. Within a year after that, I was living at the edge of Acadia National Park on Mount Desert Island in Maine—real-life landscapes that resembled those I had put together in my New York City studio apartment.

Before returning to my dissertation, I visited my luthier brother in Oregon and saw a book that he owned, *Centering*, by Mary Carolyn Richards. Since I was analyzing James Joyce's story "Clay" in *Dubliners*, I idly began to read through this book that seemed so strange, thinking it might be helpful with regard to the ptter's clay as a metaphor. I never put the book down; it took away my agony. In deep depression, as I was dismayed to discover, one feels that every cell is on fire and that you are dying, incapable of directed thinking, out of touch with God, even.

One of the things I made that summer of 1989 was an ink sketch on thick mulberry paper—of a Japanese tea hut, a mountain in the background, a rustic fence, pond, rocks, and a few grasses blowing in the wind, all quickly rendered.

I gave it the title "The Seed Garden."

Now, sixteen years later, this picture is framed and hanging over my bed in an old house in the country with a mountain behind, a pond, stone walls, grasses and wildflowers blowing in the wind. It is this farmhouse that potter Paulus Berensohn bought forty years ago to set up a studio.[10] He soon invited his friend MC Richards to share it with him; as I write this I am in what was her upstairs study. Before she died several years ago Paulus visited her at Kimberton where she had been living and teaching the disabled residents poetry, painting, and potting well into her 80s. Paulus proposed mixing her ashes with clay and making them into an unfired pot and pellets to be shared with her friends. She agreed. He brought them here to the farm in September 2001 (a few days before the disasters of 9/11). He also brought the art critic Suzi Gablik whose books I had been reading since my Oxford days and hoped someday to meet.

Some of pellets of MCs ashes mixed with clay were flung joyfully into the surrounding fields where she loved to walk while Paulus recited a favorite poem about goldenrod. Some pellets sit here in the study next to one of her pots. Some are with nearby Quaker friends Larry and Laurie who discovered this area, began to farm, and ultimately made keeping it all together possible. Some are on an altar to the Black Madonna in our friend Suzi's house in Blacksburg, Virginia. Some remain with Paulus. And a few of these pellets are in my studio, what was *their* potting studio. Clay dust still comes up from the cement floor. From the studio, I can see the clay faces MC made and nailed to the end of the big weathered barn.

I have been here five years as I write this essay. No one can see me from the road. As it turned out there are many artists in the area. It is a place of solitude, peaceful days, and fresh air in which to unpack sixty years of my life. What do I make of the fact that I am living in what I had dreamt and drawn and sculpted? As with Maine, in the 1990s, I am inhabiting a landscape that was once only a dream, a mental refuge from city surroundings, its noise and filth and sense of confinement. I do not own this haven. Yet it is mine in the sense that I seem to have created it in the imagination and made manifest my presence in it. Or rather it evolved out of who I was becoming. I will cherish this place even after I am not here. My life in this environment was "brewed" out of events I lived as if I have brewed it like a pot of tea.

ALISON ARMSTRONG

I think of the sayings of Lao Tzu that I've pinned to the door of the upstairs study that was MC's and where I write and draw and love to get snowed in: *"Produce things, cultivate things: Act without expectation...."*

The downstairs studio that was MC's and Paulus' for potting has windows in all four walls. Two overlook the giant willow and the spring and its watercress with Elk Mountain behind rolling fields; other windows look onto the hayfield that curves above the house and studio to a line of trees along the dirt road; another window and the glass door look toward the barn, the long stone wall and the remnants of an old orchard with Burt's pond beyond it and a ridge of distant mountains over which the winter sun rises and is reflected as a gold disc on the dark water; the fourth window overlooks a rock garden and steps to the house with an expanse of meadow, in summer a hayfield, in the distance, edged by the curving lane.

Who comes along that lane? A young potter, Jordan, Larry's nephew, has joined the property with a new little house, studio, and wood fired kilns he and Larry have built down behind the barn. From him perhaps I will learn new skills I crave in the perpetual search for centering. Eventually I'm drawn to the literal source of the metaphor. I have already attempted a few hand-built pieces, keeping in mind the wonderful old tea bowls I saw at the Japan Society in New York and in a book about Hamada.

It is said that when the student is ready the teacher appears. May I take it, then, that I am nearly ready, since Jordan's Stony Meadow Pottery is completed and expanding?

The first summer he was here he was making pots in a temporary workspace set up in the barn, his wheel quietly whirring in the corner where he could look out a small window onto Burt's Pond. Now he is building his second huge walk-in wood fired kiln under a canopy of corrugated tin. In the meantime, I have twenty pounds of the 35-year old stash of red clay that Paulus left in the barn. In his book, Paulus includes excerpts from his journal, in which he states that he believes he can be a potter without making pots. It is a state of being, he says.

I will think on this before I meditate again. And I will think of what the *Yoga* magazine said:

> "In contemplating the single object of meditation continually you will eventually merge with it and transcend body...and mind."

I have chosen a "support for the mind," a pink granite stone I carried with me from Maine; it has little caves and traceries like mountain paths, a place where one could live some day.

Tentatively, I've moved into an emotional or spiritual place where I may live with abandon. I do not yet know the lower geological strata of my anxiety, but I uncover it as I unpack and deal with the detritus of the decades of my life—and that of deceased parents, husband, and companion. So many things remain from my lives with them, before they died.

Simplicity seems to be within reach. Having the wood burning stove in the studio has helped immensely in this simplification process. It is not necessary to document every activity of one's past; in fact, such documentation can be a drag on the expanding energy of the present, because things all have their stories. We are so much defined by where we have been, what we have done, whom we have known, that the past sometimes seems to squeeze the present into nothing but a record of memory. But, as Alan Watts has said, the memories do not come only from the past, they are part of the present. Burning, literally and metaphorically, the no longer necessary remnants of the past are a purging gesture—as is mixing pure metaphorical charcoal, sumi mind, with a real kettle of spring water on top of the stove for yet another pot of tea.

What is not consumed by fire may be annealed in the kiln. *Anneal*— this the name Paulus gave to M C late in her life.

The word came to him before he knew what the word meant, he said. He discovered that it means to heal by fire.

MC's Swing. Photo: AA

Yesterday, a clear brilliant early autumn day. I sat in MC's old swing that Larry had made for one of her many birthdays. It hangs under the dying apple tree by her old kiln; the swing faces a break in a stone wall that opens out toward Burt's Pond. Apples fall through the branches and bounce into the grass at random intervals, missing my head. I think of Newton. And the fabled apple on his head. And of gravity.

I think of Newton and of his *Opticks* which I should finish reading for the course I'll be teaching in the city all too soon.

I begin to feel anxious. I begin not to see the pond or hear the creaking of old wood or feel the rocking of the swing.

I stop thinking.

There is a massive outcrop of rock at the other end of the pond, perfect for meditation—or a tea hut. I may never build it, but I can inhabit it in my imagination.

Perhaps that is enough, to imagine it.

I gaze at the surface of Burt's Pond, the sky and trees and mountains and grasses reflected in the surface and it, the Pond, flips into a hollow bowl of light, becomes concave.

The old red paint of the swing is faded and chipped, and splotches of grey-green lichen cover the bare wood where the old red paint has fallen away: *yugen.* It is the same lichen that grows on the stone walls and on the biggest rock by my studio door. I have photographed this lichen, would attempt to imitate it in paint; but how can you capture such simplicity and subtle shading in art? Morimoto would be able to, for he has mastered a technique using platinum prints in which the image seems to emerge from the unprimed surface of natural linen. When I was describing my readings about rainbows and ancient squabbles about how many colors are in the spectrum for the history of color theory course I teach, he told me that the Japanese have a monochrome view of the world: natural hues derived from stone, mist, moss, straw, weathered wood—along with the dark blue of indigo and the dull red of lacquer – that is his spectrum. He said that after the War when the U.S. Army bases were set up, the Japanese were astonished at the chaos of color the Americans brought: expanses of bright green lawn and the whitewashed stones used to line the edges of the roadways. It would never occur to us Japanese, he said, to paint a wall or stone or fence a color not natural to it.

Like Paulus and MC, M also taught at Haystack on Deer Isle in Maine, although I do not think they got to know each other. They are socializing in my imagination. M's art is an inspiration to me to become simple, as is his spare advice: *Make art every day. Do what is most simple.* I fail at this every day. But I begin anew. Simplicity is best. I recall Thoreau who advised this too: "Simplicity, Simplicity, Simplicity." To which his older friend Emerson responded: "One Simplicity would have sufficed."

Sen Rikyu, Tea Master

TEA

"The founders of the Way of Tea did not see things by means of convention; rather, it was their vision that brought the rules and conventions into being .... But seeing was not the sole merit of the Tea masters...for merely to see is not seeing completely. Seeing led to using, and using led to seeing still deeper...for nothing so emphasizes the beauty of things as their right application...If we want to see a thing well, we must use it well. Not only did the Tea masters enjoy beauty with the eye...they experienced it with the whole being.... To live beauty in our daily lives is the genuine Way of Tea." --Soetsu Yanagi,[11]

When the tea master invites his guests he creates an atmosphere of subdued lighting, subtle and minimal sensory stimulation. The surfaces of the tea hut and utensils are mellowed by age. Each guest must crouch, whether of high or low status in the world, to enter a small door less than three feet in height. The garden path and view of distant mountains are visible from the dim interior where water bubbles faintly in an iron kettle over a charcoal fire and the scent of a single flower soothes the air. This ephemeral structure, carefully constructed of natural materials, seems to be dissolving in Nature. Like each of us, at this moment. Here in this simple economy, this modest setting, words are an encumbrance. Conversation, like the samurai's sword in the old days, is to be left outside the small door. Here, one's inner light and the true natures of each of the guests may be perceived.

The experience is like looking at a sketch, spontaneously drawn, in which the imagination completes the full picture.

The asymmetry of some of the little tea bowls makes them seem as if made in an instant—an ideal to be achieved.

WHERE TO ART?

R, sculptor and anthropologist, after his return as visiting artist in Japan some years ago, was given one of the black T-shirts to promote the exhibition he took part it; its enigmatic legend, "Where to Art?" in red letters charmed us. We puzzled the intended meaning and finally read it as a marvelously ambiguous message, such as *Quo Vadis, Art?...* perhaps, *Where are you going, Art?* Or, *Where is art going?* Or, *Where do we go for Art?* And *Where's the Art?* Richard had asked his host to show him the best Japanese art, thinking he'd see contemporary painting. However, he was taken to a museum exhibition of ancient tea bowls. Of one, his host said, "Class One form, Class One color, Class One craftsmanship." Then, pointing out another ancient bowl, the host jumped into the air, clapped his hands once and cried out: "No craft, Spirit only! Better than Class One."

I smile to think of such enthusiasm in connection with the quiet dynamic of Tea ceremony. Although we are sitting still there is energy, alertness to the moment. Intuition is gently vibrating with the pebbles in the iron pot. In sipping the frothing tea, in sharing these moments outside chronological time, in this refined attention to detail, we are fully aware of the importance of the present; we partake of a simple harmony that transcends the ego, its willfulness, its ambitions, its anxieties. Here, we create the awareness, *a-war-e;* the life we live proceeds from the mind. And that harmony of mind manifests itself in harmony with the world.

Healing begins, then, with a well-made cup of tea sipped from a bowl that fits the palms of the hands perfectly, as it fit and was fashioned in the hands of its maker. After much study, spontaneity. Let's not even think about drinking tea made with a teabag in a plastic cup of lukewarm water sipped while reading a newspaper [or, now, cellphone] on the subway. But if we find we are doing this, let it be with the deep calm sensation of tea ceremony's cleansing ritual and the knowledge that our character now possesses the essence of Tea, no matter where we are. We smile amidst the noise and bustle and drink another type of tea altogether.

In the humble quiet of Tea, *Cha-no-yu*, the vision has been handed on, and we respond to the astonishing beauty of the inevitable unfolding of our lives. We are drinking tea we have steeped in a pot we have fashioned with water we have carried to a kettle we have boiled on a fire of wood we have hewn in a hut we have built. What we taste is tea *as* we have brewed it.

well in JAPAN

Nambo Sokei, a disciple of Sen Rikyu the great 17th century tea master, wrote the following observation:

> *Rikyu hoped further to develop his way in his conception of the manner of the tea ceremony. He sincerely sought and practiced the Way…continuously referring to the rules of Zen temples.*
>
> *He was able to modify and simplify the* shoin *style and create a pure world in a* soan *tearoom at the end of the* roji.
>
> *He lived in this humble dwelling of two mats, brought firewood and water for tea himself and came to know, though indistinctly, the true taste of a bowl of tea. His state of mind being not yet perfectly transparent, sometimes there was impurity in the water of his tea.*[12]

We cannot escape it: how we live our lives *is* the way we have of making tea.

ALISON ARMSTRONG

ADDENDUM

O VER THE COURSE of rewriting this essay my dear dog Saki has died; Old Japan boutique closed its Bleecker Street doors; Jordan has since moved his kiln and growing family to North Carolina; Larry has renovated the farm house and studio so they are less rustic; Laurie has planted more flowerbeds; our extended coterie of friends in the area has dispersed…. One little bisqued leaf shaped pot alone survives of this author's efforts at becoming a potter. And I am a full time resident again of the Greenwich Village Westbeth community, teaching literature, once again, in an art school…. Other adventures, other pursuits await more memoirs yet to be written.

Endnotes

1 *Zen Cha-no-Yu*, Daisetz T. Suzuki, *Zen and Japanese Culture* (Bollingen, 1953).

2 This is further elaborated upon in my essay "Meditations of a Lady Sea-Kayaker."

3 Alex Kerr, *Lost Japan* (Melbourne: Lonely Planet Publications, 1996; 2002)

4 *Centering: in Pottery, Poetry, and the Person* (Wesleyan Univ. Press, 1964). Also: *The Crossing Point: Selected Talks and Writings* (Wesleyan Univ. Press, 1973).

5 www.sumiya-spoon.com

6 *Memories, Dreams, Reflections* (Vintage, 1963). More recently Jung's Red Book has been published in English translation by Norton Publishing; it was on display at the Rubin Museum of Himalayan Art in Manhattan in 2009-10.

7 In lectures contained in "Out of Your Mind" from the *Alan Watts Audio Archives* (Sounds True).

8 See for example his influential 1912 work, *Concerning the Spiritual in Art* (Dover reprints).

9 (Boston: Charles E. Tuttle, 1997). See p. 80: "It is a sense of sadness, but a delightful sadness."

10 His book, *Finding One's Way with Clay* (NY: Simon & Schuster, 1972) continues to be influential.

11 *The Way of Tea* (Shambala Press, 1952).

12 Metsugo (c1704). Qtd. in D.T. Suzuki.

Endless Mountains Farm, July-September 2002;
New York City, February 2005;
New York City, June 2009;
Merigomish, Nova Scotia &
Endless Mountains Farm, June 2010.
New York City, July 2018

Printed in the United States
By Bookmasters